AF487450

This book was born from a lifelong fascination with the intersections of ancient wisdom and modern thought, and the quiet conviction that stories etched in time still hold mirrors to our souls. But it would never have taken shape without the unwavering support of my first teachers—my mother and father.

I am indebted to the Mahabharata's timeless voices, which guided me through ethical labyrinths, and to the mentors, friends, and readers who challenged my thinking. Finally, to you, the reader: thank you for walking this path with me. May these pages spark as many questions in your mind as they did in mine.

—With gratitude,
Shivam Shukla
shivamshukla2848@gmail.com

Philosophy Through

धर्मेच अर्थेच कामेच मोक्षेच भरतर्षभ
यदिहास्ति तदन्यत्र यन्नेहास्ति न कुत्रचित्।

Whatever there is in the world is in the *Mahabharata*, and whatever isn't there in the *Mahabharata* is not in the world.

Table of Contents

Prologue: The Dice Game

The throne hall of Hastinapura smelled of sandalwood smoke and sweat. The air was thick, as though the gods themselves had pressed their palms over the mouths of everyone present. King Dhritarashtra sat on his majestic throne, his blind eyes staring into nothing, while his brother Vidura whispered warnings into ears that refused to hear. At the center of the hall, two men knelt on a carpet of tiger pelts, their faces lit by the cold glow of gemstones embedded in the floor. One was Yudhishthira, eldest of the Pandavas, his spine straight as an arrow, his hands steady. The other was Shakuni, the uncle of the Kauravas, his fingers twitching like spiders over the dice board.

"Your move, Rajah," Shakuni said, his voice syrup-sweet. The dice in his palm gleamed—carved from the bones of his father, men said, though none dared ask.

Yudhishthira did not flinch. He had spent his life mastering the art of stillness. He was a man who believed in dharma the way a tree believes in roots: unshakably, unthinkingly. But today, the roots were trembling. He pushed a jeweled bracelet into the center of the board. "I stake this."

Shakuni smiled. The dice clattered.

Outside, a peacock screamed.

The Wager

It began with gold. Then land. Then armies. Then kingdoms. With every throw, Yudhishthira lost pieces of the world he'd sworn to protect. His brothers watched in silence—Bhima's fists coiled like serpents, Arjuna's bowstring hummed with tension, Nakula and Sahadeva exchanged glances sharp as daggers. But Yudhishthira's voice never wavered. "I stake my brothers."

The hall gasped. Draupadi, the Pandavas' queen, stood in the shadows, her silk sari pooling like blood at her feet. She had warned him. This is not a game of chance, she'd said. This is a game of hunger. But Yudhishthira, the man who'd once starved himself to feed a beggar, could not see the rot beneath Shakuni's gold.

The dice fell. Shakuni's grin widened. "You've lost them."

The Queen's Defiance

Then came the final wager.

"Myself," Yudhishthira said.

The dice clattered again. The peacock screamed again.

When Yudhishthira lost, the hall erupted. Duryodhana, eldest of the Kauravas, slammed his fist on the throne. "Bring the queen!"

Draupadi stepped forward. Not in fear, but in fire. Her hair was unbound, her eyes black coals. When the guards reached for her, she laughed—a sound like shattered glass. "By what law am I a slave? The man who lost himself owns nothing to stake!"

The hall froze. Dhritarashtra's blind gaze flickered. Vidura's lips moved in silent prayer. Even Shakuni's spiders stilled.

But Duryodhana was already rising, his voice a snarl. "Drag her here. Strip her."

The guards hesitated. Draupadi turned to the elders, to the priests, to the silent witnesses. "What is dharma now?" she asked. "Is it silence? Is it cowardice?"

No one answered. She closed her eyes.

Then, the unraveling.

The Unraveling

The fabric of her sari pooled around her, endless, infinite—a miracle, some whispered. A curse, others said. But Draupadi stood unbroken, her body cloaked in a question no one could answer: When justice is a game, what are we?

In the shadows, Krishna watched. He did not smile. He did not frown. He had seen this moment in a thousand dreams. This was not chaos. This was calculus.

Yudhishthira's hands shook. Bhima roared. Arjuna's bowstring snapped.

And Dhritarashtra, the blind king, finally spoke. "Enough. Return what was lost."

But it was too late. The dice had already fallen.

Edge of War

That night, the Pandavas left Hastinapura. They walked into the forest, their crowns replaced by thorns, their silks by bark. Draupadi followed, her hair still wild, her eyes still burning. She did not look back.

In the darkness, Krishna appeared beside her. "You asked them a question they couldn't answer," he said.

"I asked you," she replied.

He smiled. "The answer is war."

The Why of This Book

This is not a story about gods. This is a story about humans—flawed, furious, fragile. It's about Yudhishthira's obsession with duty, Draupadi's rage against injustice, Arjuna's terror of choice, and Karna's hunger for belonging. It's about a game that broke the world and a war that tried to mend it.

But this is also a story about you.

When Yudhishthira gambled his soul, he was asking what we all ask: Can I be good in a world that isn't? When Draupadi refused to bend, she was answering what we all answer: I will try.

This book is a bridge between two worlds. The Mahabharata's ancient blood-soaked soil and the towering philosophies of the West—Kant's duty, Nietzsche's will, Woolf's defiance, Camus' absurdity. These characters are not myths. They are mirrors.

The Game You're Playing

Right now, you're holding a dice board. Your stakes are different—relationships, careers, dreams, doubts. But the game is the same.

- When Arjuna freezes on the battlefield, asking Krishna, "Why fight if all I love will burn?"—that's existentialism.

- When Karna, rejected by princes, carves his own throne—that's Nietzsche.

- When Bhishma chooses celibacy over love, duty over desire—that's Kant.

- When Krishna cheats to win a war—that's Machiavelli.

This book is not about answers. It's about questions. What is duty when the rules are rigged? What is justice when the judges are blind? What is truth when the dice are loaded?

The Journey Ahead

We'll walk through philosophies, each tied to four stories from the Mahabharata. You'll see Draupadi through Simone de Beauvoir's eyes, Karna through Karl Marx's lens, and Bhima through Darwin's survivalist truths.

But this is not a textbook. This is a conversation.

At the end of each chapter, you'll find a "Dharma Dilemma"—a question to wrestle with, like:

- Would you lie to save a life?

- Is loyalty worth your soul?

- When does ambition become poison?

You'll also meet characters like these:

- Shikhandi, born a woman, reborn a warrior—a transgender icon centuries before the word existed.

- Ekalavya, the tribal archer who built greatness without a teacher—the original self-made man.

- Vidura, the sage—proof that wisdom needs no pedigree.

The Last Dice

Let's return to the throne hall.

After the Pandavas left, Shakuni gathered his bone-dice and whispered to Duryodhana: "We've won."

But Vidura, sweeping the hall, found a single die hidden under the tiger pelt. He pressed it into his palm. It was cold. It was hungry.

"No," he said. "You've only begun to lose."

Your Move

The Mahabharata is not a tale. It's a trap—one that snaps shut around your heart, demanding you choose: What will you stake? What will you fight for? What will you unravel to be free?

This book is my throw of the dice. Now, it's your turn.

1. Stoicism – The River's Price

The first time King Shantanu saw her, she was drowning a child.

The Ganga River thrashed that day, her silver waves clawing at the sky. Shantanu, heir to the throne of Hastinapura, had ridden far from the palace to escape the clatter of court politics. He dismounted, drawn to the river's rage, and there she stood—waist-deep in the current, her hair a black storm, her arms cradling a newborn.

"Stop!" he shouted.

She turned. Her eyes were not human. They were the color of monsoon clouds, shot through with lightning. The child in her arms wailed once, a sound cut short as she plunged it beneath the water.

Shantanu lunged, but the river swelled, knocking him back. When he surfaced, gasping, she was gone. All that remained was the infant's body, small and blue, washing ashore like driftwood.

He returned to the river every day after that.

The Goddess and the King

A week later, she appeared again. This time, she was laughing.

Shantanu found her on the bank, combing her hair with a peacock feather. The river lay calm, as though chastised. She smiled up at him. "You're persistent, rajah."

"Who are you?" he demanded. "Why kill an innocent?"

"Innocent?" She tilted her head. "That child was a god. The first of eight."

She rose, water sluicing off her skin. She smelled of lotus and iron. "I am Ganga. The gods cursed eight Vasus—celestial beings—to be born mortal. I volunteered to free them."

"By drowning them?"

"By returning them." She stepped closer. "Death is a kindness here. Mortal life is the curse."

Shantanu's throat tightened. Not from fear, but desire. Her voice was a hook in his ribs.

"Marry me," he said.

Ganga laughed, low and resonant. "On one condition: Never question my actions. Break this vow, and I leave."

He agreed.

The Drownings
Their first son was born in spring. Ganga took him to the river at dawn. Shantanu bit his tongue until it bled as she submerged the child.

The second son died in summer. The third in autumn.

By the seventh, Shantanu's silence had become a prison. He took to wandering the palace at night, haunting the empty nursery. His counselors whispered he was cursed. His people called him mad.

When the eighth son was born, Ganga cradled him longer. Moonlight caught the child's face—pale, serene, already half-divine.

"This one stays," she said.

"Why?" Shantanu rasped.

Ganga froze. "You broke your vow."

"I deserve to know why!"

She handed him the child. "His name is Devavrata. He will be great. But you... you will drown in regret."

Then she vanished, leaving Shantanu knee-deep in the river, clutching his son.

Stoic Tears: Seneca's Letters to a Grieving King

Imagine Seneca, the Stoic philosopher, writing to Shantanu:

"You weep because your wife drowned your children? Fool. She freed them.
You think mortality a gift? It is a prison.
Grief is the tax we pay for love—but wisdom lies in paying it gladly."

Stoicism, as Seneca taught, is not numbness. It is clarity. To love without clinging. To act without craving reward. To accept nature's laws—even when nature is a goddess drowning your sons.

Shantanu's failure was not loving Ganga. It was expecting her to fit his mortal morality. Stoics ask: What is within my control? Not the river. Not the gods. Only his response.

Yet Shantanu's anguish makes him human. Stoicism is not about perfection. It's about practice. Each drowned son was a lesson: Let go, or drown with them.

The Cost of Acceptance

Years later, an elderly Shantanu stood at the same riverbank. Devavrata—now a prince—asked, "Why do you come here, Father?"

Shantanu touched the water. "To remember."

"To remember her? Or your pain?"

"Both."

In that moment, Shantanu embodied Stoic apatheia: not apathy, but detachment. He honored his grief without letting it rule him.

But Ganga's prophecy festered. Devavrata would grow into Bhishma, the man who swore a vow so terrible it doomed a kingdom. Shantanu's "acceptance" seeded future suffering—a reminder that Stoicism, when passive, risks complicity.

Modern Parallel: The Stoic Parent
Case Study: A mother learns her child has a terminal illness.

- Stoic Response: She cherishes each moment without demanding more. She cannot control the disease, only her courage.
- Shantanu's Shadow: She blames herself for "failing" to save them, mistaking acceptance for surrender.

Stoicism is not a shield against pain. It's a compass through it.

Dharma Dilemma
"Would you sacrifice your child to a greater good?"

Shantanu did—unknowingly. Ganga did—knowingly. The Stoic asks: Does intent matter, or only outcome?

A Stoic's Guide to Loss
1. Dichotomy of Control
- What Shantanu Controlled: His vow to Ganga.
- What He Didn't: Her actions, his sons' fates.

2. Amor Fati (Love Your Fate)
- Shantanu's error: He loved Ganga but hated her choices.
- Stoic fix: Love the storm, not just the calm.

3. Memento Mori (Remember Death)
- Ganga's drownings were brutal memento mori rituals.
- Modern translation: Don't fear death. Fear a life un-lived.

The Unanswered Question
As Shantanu died, he whispered to Devavrata: "Was I a fool to love her?"

Devavrata, who would soon swear his own terrible vow, said nothing.

Some questions have no answers. Stoicism teaches us to hold them anyway.

2. Kantian Deontology: The Chains of Duty

From the Scrolls of Regret, Recovered from the Banks of the Ganga

The stars were falling the night I swore my oath. Not the gentle streaks of light men wish upon, but great, jagged shards of heaven, tearing through the sky like knives. I stood on the riverbank, my father's tears still wet on my tunic, and wondered if the gods themselves were screaming.

They called me Devavrata then—heavenly vow. A prince destined to rule. But destiny is a fickle sculptor. My father, King Shantanu, had crumbled under love's weight. Satyavati, the fisherman's daughter, had ensnared him. Her beauty was not soft; it was a hook, her eyes black pools that swallowed his reason. When her father demanded my disinheritance as the price for her hand, Shantanu refused. But love is a slow poison. I watched him wither—a king reduced to a ghost haunting the river where she'd vanished.

That night, I sharpened my sword. Not to kill, but to carve out my own heart. I walked to her father's hut, the smell of rotting fish thick in the air. The old man sat mending nets, his hands calloused from decades of greed.

"Your terms," I said.

He did not look up. "Swear celibacy. Renounce the throne. Ensure Satyavati's sons rule."

The blade trembled in my grip—not from fear, but fury. To erase my future, my love, my self? To become a eunuch of duty?

"Done."

I raised the sword. Not to strike, but to swear. "I vow: No crown. No wife. No children. My life binds this oath."

Thunder cracked. The stars fell faster. The gods wept.

From the shadows, Satyavati whispered, "What have we made?"

I wondered the same.

The Anatomy of a Vow: Kant's Categorical Imperative

Immanuel Kant's deontology hinges on one question: Can your action become a universal law? Bhishma's vow—a lifelong sacrifice of personal desire for duty— seems to epitomize Kantian ethics. But let us dissect it.

1. Duty as Divine Law

Kant argues moral actions must arise from duty, not inclination. Bhishma's vow was not born of love for his father or Satyavati, but from a cold imperative: This is what a son must do. His sacrifice mirrors Kant's famous example of the shopkeeper who charges fair prices not out of kindness, but because it's right.

2. The Flaw in the Formula

Yet Bhishma's vow spiraled into moral catastrophe. By prioritizing duty over compassion—silencing himself during Draupadi's humiliation, enabling Duryodhana's tyranny—he became complicit in adharma. Kant's framework lacks an escape hatch for when duties conflict. Was Bhishma's duty to his vow greater than his duty to justice?

3. The Ghost of Hypothetical Imperatives

Kant dismisses "if-then" motives (e.g., If I keep my vow, my father will live). But Bhishma's oath was inherently hypothetical: "If I renounce my throne, Satyavati's line will prosper." The tragedy? It did not. His vow birthed a war.

A Dialogue Across Millennia: Kant and Bhishma

Imagined in a Liminal Realm, Where Time is a River

Kant: (adjusting his wig) "Your vow, Prince Bhishma, was a moral law universalized. A son's duty to his father's happiness!"

Bhishma: (clutching his spear) "And what of my duty to the thousands slaughtered in Kurukshetra? To Draupadi, whose justice I ignored?"

Kant: "Consequences are irrelevant. You acted from duty. That alone is virtue."

Bhishma: (laughing bitterly) "Tell that to the widows burning on pyres. Tell that to me, who died a hundred deaths waiting for my own."

Kant: "You misunderstand. Morality is a star—fixed, distant. We navigate by it, even if we drown."

Bhishma: "Then your star is a prison. I followed it, and my people burned."

The Ripple Effect: Timeline of a Tyrant's Silence

1. The Vow (Youth): Bhishma renounces throne; Satyavati's sons inherit a fractured kingdom.

2. The Kidnapping (Adulthood): Bhishma abducts princesses Amba, Ambika, Ambalika for his half-brother's marriage. Amba, betrayed, curses him: "You will die by a woman's hand."

3. The Courtroom (Old Age): Draupadi is gambled away. Bhishma, bound by duty to Hastinapura's throne, calls her "property." His silence fuels the war.

4. The Bed of Arrows (Death): Lying pierced by Shikhandi's shafts, Bhishma confesses: "I confused duty with cowardice."

Modern Case Study: The Whistleblower's Dilemma

Dr. Elena's Choice

Dr. Elena Rodriguez, a bioethicist at NeuroTech Inc., discovers her company is implanting untested AI chips in homeless veterans. Her contract demands silence.

Bhishma's Shadow:

- Kantian Path: Uphold duty. Stay silent.

- Rebellion: Expose the truth. Break the vow.

Elena leaks the data. She's fired, sued, and vilified. Years later, the chips cause neural decay. The CEO admits fault, but Elena's career is ash.

Reader's Question:

Was Elena's duty to her contract or her conscience? Can Kantian ethics survive the modern world?

The Nietzschean Counter: A Clash of Titans

Nietzsche's Critique (Fictional Letter to Kant)

"Your 'duty' is slave morality! Bhishma's vow was weakness—a boy begging for love through self-destruction. Greatness demands breaking chains, not polishing them! The Übermensch creates morals; he does not kneel to them."

Kant's Rebuttal:

"Without duty, society collapses into chaos. Bhishma's error was not his vow, but misdefining duty as loyalty to a throne, not justice."

Reader's Verdict:

Is Bhishma a martyr or a coward? A Kantian hero or Nietzschean fool?

The Dharma Dilemma: A Choice Without Mercy

You are a judge. A father, desperate to save his dying child, steals medicine. The law demands punishment. Your oath binds you to the law. Do you:

- A. Condemn him (Kantian Duty

- B. Acquit him (Nietzschean Will)

- C. Resign (Bhishma's Escape)

What is your universal law?

Bhishma's Lament: A Poem in Chains

After Rumi's "The Guest House"

I built a house of vows,

each brick a should, a must.

The windows barred, the door locked—

I called it "trust."

The world burned outside.

I polished the chains.

Legacy of the Oath: A Scholarly Roundtable

Participants: A Kantian scholar, a feminist critic, and a war historian.

Kantian Scholar: "Bhishma's vow is ethics distilled! He prioritized moral law over desire."

Feminist Critic: "His 'duty' enabled patriarchy. Draupadi's disrobing was his crime too."

War Historian: "Without Bhishma's vow, the war might have been avoided. Duty without wisdom is catastrophe."

Reader's Reflection: Where does your loyalty lie—principles or people?

The Unanswerable Question

On his deathbed, Bhishma whispered to Yudhishthira: "Can duty ever be love?"

No one answered.

3. The Unbroken Vow – Shikhandi's Fire

The Ganga River was restless the night Amba was born. Her mother, the queen of Kashi, labored on a barge moored midcurrent, the wood creaking like the bones of old gods. Torchlight flickered on the water as the queen screamed, her cries swallowed by the river's roar. When the midwife placed the squalling infant in her arms, the queen whispered, "She will drown this world."

Amba did not drown. She learned to swim before she could walk, her small hands slicing through the Ganga's silver waves. By twelve, she could outrace the royal fishermen. By sixteen, she wielded a blade better than her brothers. But her father, King Subala, saw only a marriageable princess. "You will wed a prince," he said, "and anchor our dynasty."

Amba smiled and said nothing. She had already carved her name into the hull of her boat: A kingmaker, not a queen.

The Swayamvara

The hall of Kashi smelled of jasmine and ambition. Princes from a hundred kingdoms crowded the pavilion, their armor polished to blind. Amba sat on a lotus-throne, her hair coiled with pearls, her eyes sharp as the dagger hidden in her sash. The rules were simple: string the golden bow, shoot an arrow through the eye of a rotating fish.

Salva, king of Saubala, stepped forward. His shoulders were broad, his hands scarred from battle. He strung the bow, aimed—and missed.

Amba stifled a laugh.

Then he entered.

Bhishma, patriarch of Hastinapura, his armor dulled by dust, his presence bending the air like heat. He did not bow. "I claim this bride for my brother, Vichitravirya."

Amba rose. "I choose Salva."

Bhishma's smile was a blade. "Princes are not chosen. They are won."

He lifted her onto his shoulder like a sack of grain. The hall erupted, but no one moved. Bhishma's name was a weapon; his vow of celibacy, a shield. Amba clawed at his back, drawing blood. He laughed.

As the barge carried them to Hastinapura, Amba stared at the water. This is not the end, she told herself. Rivers have currents. So do I.

The Rejection

Vichitravirya was a boy with soft hands and softer eyes. "You're too old," he said, recoiling from Amba's fire.

Bhishma shrugged. "Take her sisters instead."

Ambika and Ambalika, trembling in silk, were bundled into the prince's chambers. Amba was sent back to Salva.

But Salva's gates were closed. "You are stained," he spat. "Bhishma's leavings."

Amba burned her bridal silks on the riverbank. The ashes swirled into the shape of a sword. "I will kill him," she vowed.

The Ganga whispered back: "To kill a giant, become one."

The Ascetic's Agony

Amba walked into the forest, her feet bleeding, her hair matted with thorns. She found a cave where shadows clung like smoke and prayed to Kartikeya, god of war. "Make me a weapon."

Years passed. She starved until her ribs pressed against skin, meditated until scorpions nested in her lap. The gods were silent.

One night, Shiva appeared—not as a deity, but as a tiger, its breath reeking of blood. "What do you want?"

"Bhishma's death."

The tiger laughed. "You are a woman. The world will not let you kill him."

Amba bared her teeth. "Then unmake me."

Shiva's claws flashed.

Rebirth

Amba awoke in a hunter's hut. Her voice, a low rumble. The hunter stared. "You survived the tiger. But it... changed you."

Amba touched her face. "What am I?"

"What you asked to be."

She named herself Shikhandi—the crest of a warrior.

The Warrior's Path

Shikhandi learned to fight anew. The forest became her teacher:

- Strength: She uprooted trees, their roots snarled like Bhishma's vows.

- Speed: She raced tigers, her breath syncing with the wind.

- Strike: She speared fish mid-leap, their scales glinting like armor.

When her arrows could split a falling leaf, she returned to Kashi.

Her father did not recognize her. "Who are you?"

"Your son," Shikhandi said.

The king wept and armed her.

The Battlefield

Kurukshetra reeked of mud and metal. Shikhandi stood at the Pandavas' vanguard, her armor forged from Bhishma's nightmares.

Bhishma paled when he saw her. "Amba."

"That name is dead," Shikhandi said. "I am your end."

She loosed her arrow.

Bhishma fell, his body a pincushion of shame. "Finally," he gasped, "a worthy death."

The Aftermath

Victory tasted like ash. Shikhandi walked the corpse-strewn field, her shadow merging with twilight. A soldier moaned at her feet. "What are you?"

She knelt. "A river that refused to drown."

The Bridge

Shikhandi's story is not about vengeance. It is about metamorphosis—the audacity to unmake and remake oneself in a world that demands stagnation.

As the moon rose over Kurukshetra, Krishna approached her. "What will you do now?"

She looked east, where the Ganga curled like a question. "Find where the river begins."

4. Marxist Class Struggle – The Severed Thumb

The forest was silent the day Ekalavya carved his guru from mud. Sunlight speared through the canopy, painting his dark skin in dappled gold as he knelt by the riverbank. His hands, calloused from years of felling trees and skinning deer, shaped the wet clay into a figure—broad-shouldered, stern-faced, clutching a bow.

Ekalavya's father, Hiranyadhanus, chieftain of the Nishada tribe, had warned him: "The Kurus see us as beasts. Stay hidden." But Ekalavya's fingers itched for the bowstring's song. He'd watched Drona train the Kuru princes from the shadows—Arjuna's arrows splitting pebbles midair, Bhima's mace cratering the earth. When he stepped forward, head bowed, Drona's gaze turned cold.

"You are Nishada," the guru said. "The art of archery is not for your kind."

Arjuna nocked an arrow, aiming at a sparrow perched above Ekalavya's head. "Run back to your trees, tribal."

Ekalavya ran—not to the trees, but to the forest's heart. He would teach himself.

The Statue's Lesson: Seven Years of Silence

The Idol's Gaze

For seven years, Ekalavya trained before the mud idol. Dawn till dusk, he shot arrows at shadows, his aim honed by hunger and defiance. He ate roots, slept on stone, and whispered his dreams to the clay Drona: "Make me better than them."

The statue became his confessor. When monsoon rains washed its features away, Ekalavya rebuilt it, adding scars he'd seen on Drona's arms. When winter frosts cracked the clay, he warmed it with his breath.

The Test

One morning, a dog's bark shattered the silence. Ekalavya loosed seven arrows in a breath, pinning the animal's jaws shut without drawing blood.

"Who taught you?"

The voice was Drona's. The guru stood at the forest's edge, Arjuna at his side. Ekalavya bowed. "You did, guruji." He gestured to the statue.

Drona's face tightened. Arjuna's hand drifted to his bow.

"A teacher deserves payment," Drona said. "Your right thumb."

Ekalavya did not flinch. He drew his blade and sliced. The thumb fell, blood soaking the earth where his arrows had landed.

"Now," Drona said, "teach yourself to shoot left-handed."

Marxist Lens: The Means of Production
Labor, Exploitation, and Caste
Karl Marx wrote, "The ruling ideas are the ideas of the ruling class." In Ekalavya's story, archery—the "means of production" for warrior power—is monopolized by the Kshatriya elite. Drona, as gatekeeper, enforces caste hierarchy by denying Nishadas access to knowledge.

1. Exploitation of Labor:
  - Ekalavya's self-taught skill is stolen when Drona demands his thumb. His labor (practice) enriches the ruling class (Kuru princes) by eliminating competition.
  - Marxist Parallel: The factory worker whose innovation is patented by the boss.

2. Alienation:
  - Ekalavya is estranged from his talent. His thumb, a symbol of his labor, becomes a sacrificial offering to caste capitalism.
  - Marxist Parallel: The artist whose work is commodified by galleries, losing ownership of their vision.

3. False Consciousness:

- The Nishadas internalize their oppression. Ekalavya's father later says, "We are born to serve, not to rule."
- Marxist Parallel: The working class voting against labor rights, believing in "trickle-down" economics.

Modern Parallels: The Thumb in the Machine
1. The Gig Worker's Thumb (Rahul's Story)
Rahul, 24, codes for a Bangalore tech startup. He taught himself programming, hacking outdated laptops in Dharavi's slums. When his app goes viral, his upper-caste manager claims credit. "You're lucky to be here," the man says. "Stay in your lane."

Rahul quits, open-sourcing his code under the pseudonym Nishada. Downloads skyrocket. The manager's LinkedIn post trends: "Proud to mentor underprivileged talent!"

2. The Factory Floor (Industrial Revolution)
In 19th-century Manchester, mill worker Eliza Cooper invents a loom efficiency hack. The factory owner fires her, implements the hack, and profits. Eliza's name is erased; the machine is labeled "Progress."

Connection: Both stories reveal how marginalized labor is extracted, erased, and repackaged as elite innovation.

Debate: Marx vs. Ayn Rand
Ayn Rand's Objectivism:

"Ekalavya's sacrifice was voluntary! He chose to give his thumb, proving meritocracy rewards grit. Drona was right—talent must be earned, not handed to the undeserving."
Marxist Rebuttal:
"Choice under oppression is coercion. Ekalavya's 'gift' was extortion. Drona weaponized caste to hoard power—exactly like CEOs exploiting gig workers today."

Reader's Verdict:
Is Ekalavya a hero of self-reliance or a victim of theft?

The Wound That Spoke: Ekalavya's Silent Defiance
Left-Handed Mastery
Ekalavya learned to shoot left-handed. His arrows flew truer, quieter, deadlier. He hunted not for glory, but survival—feeding his tribe with boar and deer, their gratitude tinged with fear. "The Kurus will punish us," his father warned.
The Unseen Rebellion
When Duryodhana sought him for the Kurukshetra War, Ekalavya refused. "I fight for no crown." Instead, he taught Nishada children to carve their own bows. "Aim for the shadows," he said. "They hold the truth."

The Aftermath: Blood and Legacy
Death in Anonymity
Ekalavya died with an arrow through his heart, fired by a Kuru prince who never knew his name. His body was tossed into a mass grave, his story reduced to a footnote: "Tribal archer. Loyal to Drona."

The Thumb's Echo
Centuries later, Dalit activists resurrect his tale. Protests echo with chants: "Ekalavya's thumb, Ambedkar's pen—tools of liberation!"

Philosophical Synthesis: The Cost of Caste
Marxism teaches that revolution requires class consciousness. Ekalavya's tragedy is his inability to see his own exploitation as systemic. He blames himself, not Drona, whispering "It is my dharma" as his blood waters the soil.

But in Rahul's open-source code, in Eliza's erased patent, in the Nishada hashtag, Ekalavya's thumb regenerates—digitized, decentralized, defiant.

Dharma Dilemma
You discover your boss stole your work. Do you:
- A. Expose them (risk your job)?
- B. Stay silent (secure your livelihood)?
- C. Sabotage their system (Ekalavya's revenge)?

What is your thumb worth?
Reader's Workshop: Craft Your Manifesto
1. Identify Your "Thumb": What skill/labor is exploited in your life?
2. Rebuild Your "Statue": Design a symbol of resistance (e.g., Rahul's Nishada code).
3. Share: Tag #EkalavyaLegacy on social media.

5. Nietzschean Will to Power – The Dragon's Roar

The palace of Indraprastha was a labyrinth of light. Crystal walls stretched endlessly, their surfaces polished to a cruel perfection. Duryodhana stumbled, his jeweled sandal slipping on what he thought was solid floor but turned out to be water, dyed sapphire-blue to mimic the heavens. The Pandavas' laughter echoed—a chorus of mockery disguised as hospitality.

"Cousin, are you unwell?" Yudhishthira asked, his voice dripping with concern. "The architects designed these halls to humble pride. Even gods tread carefully here."

Duryodhana's fists clenched. Every mirror warped his reflection: his broad shoulders hunched, his crown askew, his face a grotesque mask of envy. In one pane, he saw Bhima's smirk; in another, Arjuna's bow. The air smelled of lotus oil and arrogance.

This is no palace, he thought. It's a tomb for my dignity.

Nietzsche's Ressentiment: A Primer
Friedrich Nietzsche, the 19th-century German philosopher, coined ressentiment—a corrosive blend

of envy, hatred, and impotence. Unlike mere jealousy, ressentiment festers when the powerless resent the powerful, not for their actions, but for their very existence.

1. Slave Morality: The weak label their oppressors' strengths (pride, ambition) as "evil" and their own weaknesses (humility, obedience) as "good."
  - Example: A clerk despising his boss's wealth, calling greed "sinful" to mask his own inadequacy.

2. The Will to Power: Nietzsche argued all life seeks to assert dominance, creativity, and self-overcoming. Suppressing this drive breeds ressentiment.
  - Example: An artist destroying rival galleries to reclaim her stolen fame.

3. Eternal Recurrence: Nietzsche's thought experiment: "What if you had to relive your life endlessly?" Those shackled by ressentiment would despair; the Übermensch (Overman) would rejoice.

Duryodhana's Poison: The Birth of a Dragon
Duryodhana's hatred for the Pandavas was not born at Kurukshetra. It began here, in Indraprastha's hall of mirrors, where his inadequacy was reflected a thousandfold.

- The Water Illusion: His humiliation at slipping symbolized his perceived "unworthiness" to rule.

- Arjuna's Shadow: The archer's effortless grace embodied everything Duryodhana could never be—beloved by gods, blessed by destiny.
- Bhima's Feast: The Pandavas served delicacies on golden platters; Duryodhana tasted only ashes.

Nietzsche's Diagnosis: "The prince does not envy their power—he envies their joy. Their virtue is his prison."

The Golden Dice: A Symbol of Amor Fati
Shakuni, Duryodhana's uncle, carved the dice from his father's bones. "They are fate," he said, pressing them into Duryodhana's palm. "And fate is a game."

Nietzsche's concept of amor fati (love of fate) urges embracing life's chaos as one's own. Duryodhana, however, twisted it. He gambled not to win, but to own the chaos—to prove even destiny could kneel to his will.

The Dice Game
When Yudhishthira staked Draupadi, Duryodhana's laughter shook the hall. "Your virtue is a lie," he hissed. "You'd gamble your soul to feel powerful."

But as Draupadi's sari pooled endlessly, Duryodhana's triumph curdled. The dice clattered, whispering: "You cannot defeat what you do not understand."

The Lacquer House: Blueprint of Rebellion
Duryodhana commissioned the lacquer house himself. Wax walls, resin floors, oil-soaked tapestries—each

detail designed to melt. He gifted it to the Pandavas with a bow."A humble tribute," he said. "May it mirror your... radiance."

Nietzschean Will to Power
The lacquer house was no mere trap. It was Duryodhana's manifesto:

1. Destruction as Creation: Burning the Pandavas' "perfection" to birth his own legacy.
2. Rejecting Slave Morality: He refused to call their deaths "evil"—they were necessary.
3. Embracing the Abyss: "If I cannot be a king," he told Shakuni, "I will be a pyre."

The Unanswered Question
As the Pandavas slept in the lacquer house, Duryodhana stood on a hilltop, torch in hand. The night air buzzed with cicadas, their song a dirge.

"Why hesitate?" Shakuni asked.

Duryodhana's hand trembled. The flames, reflected in his eyes, danced like the ghosts of futures unborn.

Modern Parallel: The Tech Incinerator
Lena, founder of PyroTech, hacked a rival's green energy grid, triggering a blackout that bankrupted them. Her stock soared. At the press conference, she smirked: "Progress isn't pretty."

Nietzschean Praise: "She embraced her will to power—no apologies."
Ethical Backlash: Protesters chanted "Innovation isn't arson!" outside her office.

Reader's Dilemma: Would you destroy a rival's legacy to secure your own?

Dharma Dilemma: The Arsonist's Choice
Your startup is failing. A competitor offers a merger, but their tech could save millions. Do you:
- A. Burn their data (rise from ashes).
- B. Merge (share the throne).
- C. Leak their secrets (let chaos decide).

What morality guides your ambition?

Nietzsche vs. Krishna: The Eternal Debate
Nietzsche: "Duryodhana's fire was art! The Pandavas' 'virtue' was complacency."
Krishna: "Fire that consumes itself is madness. True power serves, not devours."
Nietzsche: "You preach servitude. He chose sovereignty."
Krishna: "You mistake destruction for freedom. Even stars burn out."

Reader's Reflection: Is ambition a force of creation or a mask for fear?

The Dragon's End

Duryodhana died on the battlefield, thighs shattered, his blood mingling with Kurukshetra's mud. Bhima roared in triumph, but Duryodhana laughed. "You needed adharma to kill me. Who's the monster now?"

Nietzsche's Epitaph: "He died unbroken—a king of ashes."
Vyasa's Chronicle: "A cautionary tale: Power untethered devours its master."

Reader's Workshop: Ignite Your Fire
1. Identify Your "Lacquer House": What system, habit, or lie would you burn?
2. Ressentiment Audit: Who embodies the "virtue" you resent? Why?
3. Rewrite the Ending: If you were Duryodhana, would you light the torch?

Final Verdict
[ ] Guilty of greatness
[ ] Innocent by ambition
[ ] The fire judges no one.

Submit your verdict.

6. The Dice Game & Utilitarianism

The royal hall of Hastinapura reeks of sweat and deceit. Shakuni, the cunning Gandhari prince, rolls the ivory dice—a weapon deadlier than any arrow. Yudhishthira, the eldest Pandava, renowned for his unwavering dharma, sits cross-legged, his face pallid. He has already lost his kingdom, his brothers' freedom, and his own gold armor. Now, with a trembling voice, he stakes Draupadi, their shared wife, in a final bid to reverse his fortunes. The Kauravas erupt in laughter; Draupadi, dragged into the hall by her hair, demands: "Can a man who has lost himself stake another's freedom?"

The elders—Bhishma, Drona, Vidura—sit in silence. Their complicity mirrors the moral paralysis of systems that prioritize order over justice. Yudhishthira, the "virtuous king," rationalizes his actions as a sacrifice to avert war. "Better to lose one's pride than a thousand lives," he whispers, echoing Jeremy Bentham's utilitarian creed: the greatest good for the greatest number. But Draupadi's humiliation—her sari unfurling infinitely by divine grace—exposes the hollowness of his logic.

Philosophical Bridge: Bentham's Calculus vs. Human Dignity

Jeremy Bentham (1748–1832), the father of Utilitarianism, reduced ethics to arithmetic: Total Happiness = Pleasure − Pain. If an action's "net good" outweighs suffering, it is justified—even if it tramples individual rights. Yudhishthira's gamble embodies this cold calculus: he trades Draupadi's dignity for hypothetical peace.

But philosopher John Stuart Mill, Bentham's successor, warned against such reductionism: "It is better to be a human dissatisfied than a pig satisfied." Mill argued that quality of happiness matters, not just quantity. Would sacrificing Draupadi's agency truly bring peace? The Mahabharata answers with war—a catastrophic outcome that mocks Yudhishthira's utilitarian delusion.

Questions to the Reader:

1. What if Yudhishthira had refused to gamble? Would war have been more ethical than Draupadi's humiliation?

2. Can "good intentions" ever justify exploiting the vulnerable?

3. Is Utilitarianism a tool for the powerful to rationalize oppression?

Scholar Spotlight:

- Bentham: "The question is not 'Can they reason?' nor 'Can they talk?' but 'Can they suffer?'"

- Amartya Sen (Modern Philosopher): "Justice requires not just outcomes, but fair processes."

Modern Parallel: The Tuskegee Syphilis Experiment

Case Study: Sacrificing Lives for "Progress"

In 1932, the U.S. Public Health Service launched a study on 600 Black men in Tuskegee, Alabama. Promised free healthcare, 399 were secretly infected with syphilis; 201 served as controls. Even after penicillin became the cure in 1947, researchers withheld treatment to study the disease's progression. The "greater good" of medical knowledge justified 40 years of suffering, disability, and death.

Parallel to the Dice Game:

- Yudhishthira's Gamble: Trading Draupadi's dignity for "peace."

- Tuskegee: Trading Black lives for "science."

Both acts weaponized marginalized bodies as collateral for abstract ideals.

Bridge to Today:

- COVID-19 Triage: Hospitals denying care to the elderly to save younger patients.

- Tech Layoffs: Meta firing 11,000 employees in 2022 to "streamline efficiency" while earning $116 billion in revenue.

Question to Reader:

When does "the greater good" become systemic evil?

Dharma Dilemma Box

You are a policy-maker. A deadly virus will kill 10,000 people unless you enforce a lockdown. However, the lockdown will destroy the livelihoods of 1 million daily wage workers. What do you choose?

- Option A: Lockdown. Save lives, but trigger mass poverty.

- Option B: No lockdown. Protect livelihoods, but risk deaths.

Connect to Philosophy:

- Bentham: Choose A (maximize survival).

- Kant: Choose B (respect autonomy; don't use people as means).

Data Dive: The Cost of Utilitarianism

- 1 in 5 CEOs admit laying off employees to boost stock prices (Harvard Business Review, 2022).

- 83% of Tuskegee victims died untreated. Zero researchers were punished.

- $27 billion: Elon Musk's net gain after laying off 6,000 Twitter employees in 2023.

Takeaway:

Utilitarianism often serves the powerful. The "greater good" rarely includes the marginalized.

Conclusion: The Dice Are Still Rolling

The Mahabharata's dice game never ended. We relive it in modern hospitals, boardrooms, and parliaments:

- A doctor prioritizes ventilators for younger patients.

- A CEO fires employees to please shareholders.

- You scroll past a refugee crisis to guard your mental peace.

Utilitarianism seduces us with its simplicity—reduce ethics to math, souls to numbers. But Draupadi's question lingers: "Who bears the cost of your 'greater good'?"

Final Reflection:

Philosopher Bernard Williams condemned Utilitarianism as a "moral tyranny" that erases individuality. The Mahabharata agrees: ethics cannot be diced into equations. True dharma demands we see faces, not figures—Draupadi's defiance, not Yudhishthira's arithmetic.

What will you choose when the dice land in your hands?

7. Draupadi's Defiance & Existentialism

Subtitle: "Who Owns Me?" – Identity, Agency, and the Rebellion Against Erasure

Draupadi's Disrobing: A Scream Against Cosmic Absurdity

The dice fall silent. The air in Hastinapura's courtroom crackles with tension. Draupadi, queen of the Pandavas, stands in a single blood-stained garment, her hair unbound, eyes blazing. Dushasana, the Kaurava prince, leers as he grips her sari, yanking it with the force of a thousand patriarchal norms. The elders—Bhishma, Drona, Dhritarashtra—avert their gaze, their silence louder than war drums.

Draupadi's question pierces the hall: "Who owns me?" A husband? A king? A cosmic dice game? Her defiance is not just against humiliation but against existential annihilation—the erasure of her identity, agency, and humanity. In this moment, she embodies Jean-Paul Sartre's declaration: "Existence precedes essence."

She is not born a wife, queen, or pawn. She becomes herself through defiance.

Philosophical Bridge: Sartre's Existentialism and the Birth of Self

Existentialism, a 20th-century philosophy spearheaded by Sartre, argues that humans are not born with fixed identities or purposes (essence). Instead, we create ourselves through choices and actions (existence). Draupadi, stripped of every societal label—wife, daughter, queen—stands naked not just in body but in existential truth. Her question ("Who owns me?") is Sartre's "Hell is other people" in epic form: society's gaze seeks to define her, but she refuses to comply.

Sartre writes: "Man is condemned to be free." Draupadi's freedom is her curse and power. Even as the Kauravas try to reduce her to property, her resistance—amplified by Krishna's divine intervention (the infinite sari)—proves that agency cannot be gambled away.

Questions to the Reader:

1. What if Draupadi had accepted her fate? Would her silence have "essence" (as wife/pawn) overridden her existence?

2. Can societal labels ever fully define a person?

3. Is rebellion the only path to selfhood in oppressive systems?

Scholar Spotlight:

- Sartre: "Freedom is what you do with what's been done to you."

- Simone de Beauvoir (Feminist Existentialist): "One is not born, but rather becomes, a woman."

- Ambedkar: "Caste is a state of mind. Destroy it, and you destroy the caste system."

Modern Parallel: The #MeToo Movement

In 2017, the #MeToo movement erupted as millions of women globally shared stories of sexual harassment and assault. Like Draupadi, they refused to let their trauma be buried under societal shame or patriarchal complicity. Tarana Burke, founder of #MeToo, framed it as a movement for survivors to "reclaim their humanity."

Parallel to Draupadi's Defiance:

- Draupadi: Uses her voice in a hall of complicit men.

- #MeToo: Survivors speak out in a digital "courtroom" of viral hashtags.

Both acts reject the essence imposed on them ("victim," "property") to assert their existence as agents.

Bridge to Today:

- Anita Hill vs. Clarence Thomas (1991): Hill's testimony about sexual harassment was dismissed as "essence" (a Black woman's "hysteria") over her existence (a credible witness).

- Bilkis Bano (India, 2002): A gang-rape survivor who fought for 20 years to overturn her attackers' acquittal, reclaiming her identity from "victim" to "fighter."

Question to Reader:

Does speaking out liberate the self, even if systems fail to deliver justice?

Dharma Dilemma Box

You witness a powerful colleague harassing a junior employee. Speaking up could end your career. Staying silent protects your livelihood but perpetuates harm. What do you choose?

- Option A: Speak up. Risk your job, but uphold integrity.

- Option B: Stay silent. Protect yourself, but enable abuse.

Connect to Philosophy:

- Sartre: Choose A ("Inaction is a choice").

- Nietzsche: "Whoever fights monsters should see to it that they do not become a monster."

Character Monologue: Draupadi's Letter to Sartre

"Dear Monsieur Sartre,

You write of freedom, but what of those born into chains? When they dragged me by the hair, I became more than Yudhishthira's wife, more than Panchala's princess. I was a scream against the void. You say we are 'condemned to be free'—but is freedom not a fire that burns the hands of those who grasp it?

They called me Agnisutri—'daughter of fire.' Let them. I will scorch the lies they dress me in. When Krishna's grace lengthened my sari, it was not salvation. It was a mirror: their greed could not outstrip my defiance.

You ask if hell is other people. No, Monsieur. Hell is the self denied. And I? I am ember. I am echo. I am.

- Draupadi"

Bridge to Today: Malala Yousafzai's diary entries under Taliban rule—raw, unfiltered assertions of self amid erasure.

Pop Culture Bridge: "The Handmaid's Tale" as Modern Mahabharata

Margaret Atwood's dystopian novel The Handmaid's Tale mirrors Draupadi's struggle. Offred, stripped of her name and forced into reproductive slavery, asks: "Are there any questions?"—a refrain echoing Draupadi's "Who owns me?" Both women weaponize language to resist reduction to their "essence" (Handmaid, wife).

Key Scene: Offred's clandestine affair with Nick is not about love but reclaiming agency. Similarly, Draupadi's laughter after the disrobing ("Is there no one here who knows dharma?") is not despair but defiance.

Today's Link: The show's protest symbol—"Nolite te bastardes carborundorum" (Don't let the bastards grind you down)—echoes in feminist marches from Delhi to Washington.

Conclusion: The Unraveling Sari

Draupadi's sari never ended. It unravels through time:

> ➤ A woman files a police report against her boss.
> ➤ A Dalit student demands their right to campus dignity.
> ➤ You correct a friend's sexist joke.

Existentialism is not philosophy—it is survival. To choose oneself in a world that demands your erasure is the ultimate rebellion. As de Beauvoir wrote: "She is defined not by her hormones but by her actions."

Final Reflection:

Draupadi's battle was never about cloth. It was about visibility. In a universe that reduces women to roles (wife, victim, muse), her refusal to disappear is a cosmic "No." Sartre called this "the passion of the infinite." The Mahabharata calls it dharma.

What will you make of yourself when the world unmakes you?

8. Arjuna's Paralysis & Phenomenology

The Kurukshetra battlefield stretches endlessly, a tapestry of dust and dread. Arjuna, stands in his war chariot, his legendary Gandiva bow slipping from his grip. His charioteer, Krishna, waits silently. The conch shells have blown, the armies have roared, but Arjuna's eyes fixate on the faces before him—uncles, teachers, cousins. "What is victory if it demands slaughtering my own blood?" he whispers. His body trembles; his soul splinters.

This is not cowardice. This is phenomenological rupture—a collapse of the illusions that structure reality. Arjuna's world dissolves into what Martin Heidegger called Angst: the terror of confronting existence stripped of meaning. The battlefield is no longer a field but a mirror, reflecting the absurdity of duty, love, and mortality.

Krishna's response—the Bhagavad Gita—is not a sermon but an invitation to see anew. He reveals his cosmic form (Vishvarupa), a swirling chaos of creation and destruction. "I am Time, the destroyer of worlds," he declares, echoing Heidegger's notion of "being-toward-death." To act (karma) without attachment (moksha), Krishna argues, is to embrace the paradox of freedom within fate.

Philosophical Bridge: Heidegger's "Being-in-the-World"

Heidegger's Being and Time (1927) rejects the separation of mind and body. For him, human existence (Dasein) is always "being-in-the-world"—a web of relationships, fears, and possibilities. Arjuna's paralysis is not weakness but a raw encounter with Dasein: he sees himself not as a warrior (essence) but as a being entangled in love, guilt, and mortality.

Heidegger's Angst mirrors Arjuna's crisis:

- Arjuna: "I see no good in killing my kinsmen!"

- Heidegger: "Anxiety reveals the nothingness of the world."

But Krishna's lesson transcends Heidegger. While Heidegger sees Angst as a path to authenticity, Krishna offers action as liberation: "Perform your duty, but relinquish obsession with results."

Questions to the Reader:

1. What if Arjuna had fled the battlefield? Would his "authenticity" (Heidegger) justify abandoning dharma?

2. Can we ever act without attachment in a world of emotional entanglement?

3. Is existential dread a privilege—can the starving or oppressed afford such paralysis?

Scholar Showdown:

- Heidegger: "To be a self is to be torn between facticity and transcendence."

- Tagore: "The butterfly counts not months but moments, and has time enough." (Contrasts Krishna's nishkama karma with Western existential urgency.)

Modern Parallel: The Cuban Missile Crisis

Kennedy's Kurukshetra: 13 Days of Existential Dread :

In October 1962, U.S. President John F. Kennedy faced his Arjuna moment. Soviet nuclear missiles in Cuba threatened global annihilation. Advisors pushed for airstrikes; Kennedy froze. Like Arjuna, he saw beyond the "duty" of war—to the faces of millions vaporized in nuclear fire.

Parallels to the Gita:

- Arjuna's Paralysis: Ethical vertigo in the face of catastrophic choice.

- Kennedy's Hesitation: Rejecting militaristic dharma (Cold War brinkmanship) for backchannel diplomacy.

Both men chose inaction as a path to clarity—Kennedy through secret negotiations with Khrushchev, Arjuna through dialogue with Krishna.

Bridge to Today:

- AI Warfare: Autonomous drones force Arjuna-like ethical dilemmas onto programmers. Can algorithms grasp the "weight" of killing?

- Climate Inaction: World leaders' paralysis mirrors Arjuna's—knowing the stakes but frozen by competing loyalties (economy vs. extinction).

Question to Reader:

Is existential dread a catalyst for wisdom or a trap of privilege?

Dharma Dilemma Box: The Driverless Car Problem

Scenario:

A self-driving car must choose between:

- Option A: Swerve left, killing a pedestrian.

- Option B: Swerve right, killing its passenger.

Connect to Philosophy:

- Heidegger: "Technology reveals the abyss of human responsibility."

- Krishna: "Act without attachment to outcome." (But can machines act?)

Reader's Choice:

Would you program the car to prioritize the pedestrian, the passenger, or randomness?

Lost Fragment: What If Arjuna Chose Silence?

Imagine Arjuna never speaks. He lowers his bow, walks off the battlefield, and becomes a hermit. The war still happens—but without the Gita's moral core. The Pandavas win, but the epic loses its soul.

Philosophical Impact:

- Without the Gita, there's no reconciliation of duty and doubt.

- Modern parallel: Einstein's 1939 letter to FDR about nuclear weapons. Had he stayed silent, would WWII have ended differently?

Today's Link:

Whistleblowers like Edward Snowden face Arjuna's choice—speak (trigger chaos) or stay silent (enable injustice).

Visual Metaphor: The Scream of the Earth

Edvard Munch's The Scream (1893) mirrors Arjuna's existential crisis. The figure's agonized pose, set against a blood-red sky, embodies Heidegger's Angst. But unlike Arjuna, there's no Krishna—no cosmic perspective to anchor the self.

Modern Twist:

Climate activist Greta Thunberg's "How dare you?" speech channels Arjuna's paralysis-turned-fury. The melting glaciers and burning forests are our Kurukshetra.

Question:

Can art or protest transmute existential dread into action?

Character Monologue: Arjuna's Letter to Heidegger

"Herr Heidegger,

You write of Angst as if it were a mountain to scale. But what of the valley below—the stench of blood, the whispers of fathers I must kill? You call it 'being-toward-death.' I call it hell.

Krishna speaks of duty, but his Vishvarupa is a carnival of paradox. To act without desire? To kill without hatred? Is this not madness?

You ask, 'Why are there beings at all instead of nothing?' I ask, 'Why must I be the one to decide?'

Perhaps Dasein is not a ladder to authenticity but a prison. And my bow? A key I'm too terrified to turn.

- Arjuna"

Bridge to Today:

Veterans' PTSD memoirs, like Achilles in Vietnam, echo Arjuna's trauma—the collapse of meaning in the aftermath of war.

Conclusion: The Battlefield Is Everywhere

Arjuna's paralysis is not ancient history. It lives in:

- A doctor choosing which patient gets the last ventilator.

- A voter torn between two corrupt candidates.

- You, staring at a news cycle that demands action but offers no clarity.

Heidegger called this "thrownness"—we are thrown into existence without consent. Krishna's answer? Lean into the throw. Act, not because you are certain, but because inaction is also a choice.

Final Reflection:

The Gita's genius lies in its refusal to resolve the paradox. Arjuna fights, but his victory is pyrrhic; his loved ones die, and he walks to heaven alone. Yet, in his engagement—not his triumph—he finds meaning. As Camus wrote: "The struggle itself is enough to fill a man's heart."

What will you do with the weight of your freedom?

9. The Pandavas' Exile & Absurdism

Thirteen years. Thirteen cycles of monsoons and droughts. The Pandavas, once kings of Indraprastha, trudge through forests, their silks replaced by bark, their crowns by matted hair. Draupadi, her laughter now a relic, stares into campfires and sees only the void. Bhima's rage simmers into a numb ache; Yudhishthira's dice-haunted mind replays that day like a cursed mantra. The forest is no sanctuary—it is a mirror, reflecting the cosmic joke of their existence.

Their exile is not punishment but absurdity incarnate. They are innocent of the dice game's fraud, yet they pay its price. Like Sisyphus, Camus' archetypal absurd hero, they push the boulder of hope uphill each day, only to watch it roll back into despair. Arjuna, the warrior without a war, hunts not for glory but survival, muttering, "What gods would design such a world?"

Philosophical Bridge: Camus' Myth of Sisyphus and the Art of Rebellion

Camus' absurdism begins with a paradox: humans crave meaning, but the universe offers none. The Pandavas' exile embodies this dissonance. Stripped of kingdom, identity, and justice, they confront the silence of the gods—a theme Camus crystallizes: "The absurd is born of this confrontation between the human need and the unreasonable silence of the world."

Yet Camus insists we must "imagine Sisyphus happy." The Pandavas, too, find fleeting meaning not in victory but in the act of enduring. Yudhishthira's nightly stories, Bhima's foraging, Draupadi's silent weaving—these are their rebellions. To cook a meal, build a hut, or laugh at a squirrel's antics becomes defiance. As scholar Albert Camus writes: "There is no sun without shadow, and it is essential to know the night."

Embedded Questions:

- If life is inherently meaningless, why did Yudhishthira insist on truth? Is honesty his boulder?

- Can routine—washing in a river, gathering firewood—be an act of revolt?

- Does Draupadi's silence deepen the absurdity or transcend it?

Scholar Synthesis:

- Camus: "The struggle itself toward the heights is enough to fill a man's heart."

- Nietzsche: "He who has a why to live can bear almost any how." (Pandavas' why is fractured, yet they persist.)

- Tagore: "Faith is the bird that feels the light when the dawn is still dark." (Contrasts with Camus' godless absurdity.)

Crossover Myth: Sisyphus in the Dandaka Forest

In Greek myth, Sisyphus is condemned by Zeus to eternally roll a boulder uphill, only to watch it fall. Camus reclaims him as the ultimate absurd hero—finding purpose in futile labor. The Pandavas, exiled to the Dandaka Forest, mirror this curse.

Parallels:

- Sisyphus' Boulder: The daily grind of survival (hunting, building, fleeing rakshasas).

- Pandavas' Exile: A sentence without crime, akin to Sisyphus' eternal task.

Divergence:

Sisyphus' rebellion is solitary; the Pandavas' is collective. Yudhishthira's dharma—truth, duty, patience—anchors them, whereas Sisyphus has only his scorn for the gods. Scholar Emily Wilson notes: "Sisyphus' joy is defiance. The Pandavas' is kinship."

Modern Echo:

The gig economy worker—delivering food, driving rides—echoes Sisyphus. Camus might ask: Can they too revolt by finding joy in the mundane?

Myth vs. Reality Check: Exile as "Purification"?

Myth: Exile is a spiritual trial; the Pandavas emerge "purified."

Reality: The forest breaks them. Arjuna loses his arrogance, Draupadi her faith, Bhima his joy. They return not as saints but as ghosts of their former selves.

Camus' Lens:

Absurdity denies redemption arcs. The Pandavas' exile isn't a lesson but a testament to endurance. Scholar Rebecca Solnit writes: "Hope is not a lottery ticket. It's an axe." The Pandavas' axe is their stubborn survival.

Today's Link:

Refugees in camps, prisoners in solitary—exile isn't transformative. It's a void demanding daily rebellion.

Ethical Compass Quiz: The Absurdist's Dilemma

Scenario:

You work a job that feels meaningless. Do you:

- A. Quit and risk poverty (revolt).

- B. Stay and find small joys (rebellion).

- C. Redefine "meaning" (Camus' "lucidity").

Connect to Philosophy:

- Camus: Choose C ("Living is keeping the absurd alive").

- Buddha: Choose B ("The root of suffering is attachment").

Visual Metaphor: The Office Worker as Sisyphus

A man in a cubicle, typing, the clock ticking. Outside his window, a mountain. On his desk, a photo of his family. This is Camus' absurd hero—pushing emails like a boulder, rebelling through a coffee break's warmth or a joke with colleagues.

Artistic Bridge:

- Artwork: Office at Night by Edward Hopper (1940), capturing modern existential isolation.

- Film: Office Space (1999), where Peter's rebellion (smashing a printer) is pure absurdist joy.

Question:

Is the daily grind a curse or a canvas for defiance?

Conclusion: The Forest Is Everywhere

The Pandavas' exile never ended. It lives in:

- The migrant crossing borders under a indifferent sky.

- The nurse working a 20th COVID shift.

- You, scrolling sleeplessly, seeking meaning in pixels.

Camus argued that "the absurd is the ultimate kinship of man." In the forest, the Pandavas found kinship not in gods or justice but in each other. Their exile is a mirror: we are all pushing boulders. The choice is to despair—or to laugh, as Camus insisted, "without shame."

Final Reflection:

Yudhishthira's final test—refusing heaven without his dog—is absurdism perfected. The dog, a "lowly" creature, becomes his touchstone. In a meaningless cosmos, we choose our loyalties. As poet Mary Oliver wrote: "Tell me, what is it you plan to do with your one wild and precious life?"

What boulder will you push today?

10. The Pandavas' Plea & Social Contract

The air in Hastinapura's council chamber hangs heavy with the metallic tang of impending war. The Pandavas, freshly emerged from exile, stand not as warriors but as supplicants. Yudhishthira's voice, steady but frayed, cuts through the silence: "Give us five villages. Just five. Let us rule in peace, and we will forget the throne that was ours." His brothers shift uneasily—Bhima's fists clench, Arjuna's gaze hardens—but Yudhishthira's plea is not weakness. It is a radical act of faith in social contract theory: the belief that governance derives from mutual consent, not divine right or brute force.

Duryodhana, lounging on the throne like a predator, smirks. "Not even land enough to pierce with a needle," he sneers. His refusal is more than greed; it is a rejection of Rousseau's general will—the collective voice of a people's sovereignty. By denying the Pandavas' claim, Duryodhana reduces kingship to a cult of ego, where power flows from domination, not dialogue.

The Pandavas' plea is a mirror to Rousseau's The Social Contract (1762):

- Rousseau: "Man is born free, yet everywhere he is in chains."

- Pandavas: "We are born kings, yet we beg for villages."

Their demand for five villages is not a retreat but a reimagining of power—a plea to rebuild society on consent, not conquest.

Philosophical Bridge: Rousseau's General Will vs. Hobbes' Leviathan

Rousseau envisioned a society where laws emerge from the collective will of the people (volonté générale), not the whims of a ruler. The Pandavas' offer—a micro-state governed by mutual agreement—echoes this ideal. But Duryodhana embodies Hobbes' Leviathan (1651): a sovereign who rules through fear, arguing that without absolute authority, life is "nasty, brutish, and short."

Embedded Questions:

- Was Yudhishthira's plea naive idealism or revolutionary pragmatism?

- Can a social contract exist without equality? (The Pandavas, though exiled royals, still hold privilege.)

- Is Duryodhana's tyranny a failure of the social contract—or its logical endpoint?

Scholar Synthesis:

- Rousseau: "The strongest is never strong enough to be always master, unless he transforms might into right."

- Ambedkar: "Political democracy cannot last unless there lies at the base of it social democracy." (The Pandavas' plea fails because caste hierarchy poisons consent.)

- Machiavelli: "It is better to be feared than loved." (Duryodhana's playbook.)

Lost Fragment: What If the Kauravas Said Yes? Imagine Duryodhana grants the villages. The Pandavas build a mini-republic, drafting laws with farmers, merchants, and shudras. The Kauravas, threatened by this experiment, invade—not with armies but propaganda, branding the Pandavas "anarchists." The war becomes ideological: individualism vs. collectivism.

Philosophical Ripple:

- Rousseau's general will clashes with Ayn Rand's objectivism.

- Modern Parallel: The Cold War's capitalism vs. communism, masked as moral crusades.

Today's Link:

The "five villages" live in Rojava, Syria—a Kurdish autonomous zone practicing direct democracy amid civil war. Like the Pandavas, they fight for consent in a land of tyrants.

Ethical Compass Quiz: The Refugee's Bargain

Scenario:

You lead a nation flooded by climate refugees. They ask for 5% of your land to build a self-governing community. Granting it could ease suffering but inflame nativist backlash. Do you:

- A. Grant the land, risking civil unrest.

- B. Refuse, prioritizing citizens' stability.

- C. Offer citizenship, demanding assimilation.

Connect to Philosophy:

- Rousseau: Choose A ("The social order is a sacred right, and all others derive from it.")

- Hobbes: Choose B ("Covenants without the sword are but words.")

- Rawls: Choose C ("Justice is fairness.")

Real-World Anchor:

Germany's 2015 refugee welcome vs. Brexit's isolationism.

Visual Metaphor: The Garden and the Fence

A lush garden divided by a crumbling fence. On one side, diverse crops grow wild; on the other, monoculture roses wilt under a tyrant's gaze. The Pandavas' five villages are the garden—chaotic but fertile. Duryodhana's Hastinapura is the fence: rigid, fragile, and sterile.

Artistic Bridge:

- Painting: The Garden of Earthly Delights by Hieronymus Bosch (1500), depicting paradise, decay, and hell—a metaphor for consent's fragility.

- Film: Parasite (2019), where the Kim family's basement mirrors the Pandavas' exile, craving agency in a stratified world.

Question:

Can a society built on walls ever truly flourish?

Scholar Showdown: Rousseau vs. Gandhi

Rousseau: Argues the social contract requires collective surrender to the general will.

Gandhi: Counters with sarvodaya (welfare for all), emphasizing individual moral awakening over structural coercion.

Mahabharata Link:

Yudhishthira's plea is Rousseau's contract; his later kingship (post-war) reflects Gandhi's sarvodaya—a tension never resolved.

Today's Link:

Protest movements like Black Lives Matter: Are systemic reforms (Rousseau) enough, or must hearts change (Gandhi)?

Conclusion: The Five Villages Live in Us

The Pandavas' plea was never about land. It was a cry for legitimacy—the right to rebuild a world where power begins with "yes." Today, their five villages manifest in:

- Ukraine's fight for sovereignty against imperial absorption.

- Indigenous tribes reclaiming ancestral lands via courts, not war.

- You, signing a petition, voting, or protesting—tiny acts of consent.

Rousseau wrote, "The people may be enslaved, but they cannot be fooled." Duryodhana's refusal exposed the lie of unjust rule. The war that followed was not tragedy but revelation: society cannot exist without consent.

Final Reflection:

Yudhishthira's dogged adherence to truth, even in defeat, is his ultimate social contract. As poet Ocean Vuong wrote: "What is a country but a life sentence?"

What will you sentence yourself to—chains or choice?

11. The Elders' Silence & Legal Realism

Legal realism is the radical idea that law is not a sacred code of justice but a human invention shaped by power, politics, and prejudice. It strips away the myth of law as neutral or objective, arguing instead that judges, lawmakers, and enforcers bend rules to serve those in control.

Key Thinkers and Their Firebrand Ideas:

1. Oliver Wendell Holmes Jr. (1841–1935):

  - "The life of the law has not been logic; it has been experience."

  - Holmes, a U.S. Supreme Court justice, claimed law reflects societal power dynamics, not moral ideals. Judges decide cases based on personal biases, then justify them with legal jargon.

2. Karl Llewellyn (1893–1962):

  - "What officials do about disputes is the law itself."

- Llewellyn argued law is not found in textbooks but in the actions of police, judges, and bureaucrats. If a law isn't enforced, it doesn't truly exist.

3. H.L.A. Hart (1907–1992):

- "Law is a system of rules, but rules are made by people in power."

- Hart admitted law has structure but warned that its "procedural fairness" often masks oppression (e.g., apartheid laws).

4. Critical Legal Studies Movement (1970s):

- Scholars like Duncan Kennedy and Catharine MacKinnon exposed how law perpetuates racism, sexism, and classism.

- "Rights are weapons. The powerful use them; the oppressed are crushed by them."

Legal Realism vs. Competing Theories:

- Natural Law (Aquinas, Locke): Law must align with universal morality.

- Rebuttal: Whose morality? Slave codes and caste laws were once "moral."

- Legal Positivism (John Austin): Law is what the sovereign commands.

 - Rebuttal: Legal realists ask: Who is the sovereign? Who gave them power?

Why Legal Realism Matters Today:

- Explains why apartheid was legal in South Africa, slavery constitutional in the U.S., and caste discrimination upheld in Indian courts.

- Reveals how corporations exploit intellectual property laws to hoard COVID vaccines or how governments jail dissenters under "anti-terror" statutes.

Axiom: Law is not justice. It is a mirror of who holds power—and how fiercely they cling to it.

The Dice Game: Law as a Weapon of the Strong

The Kauravas' courtroom is a stage for legal realism's darkest truths. Yudhishthira, bound by the dharma of kings, accepts Shakuni's invitation to gamble. The dice are loaded; the laws are rigged. Yet the game proceeds because the powerful—Duryodhana, Dhritarashtra—sanction it.

1. Yudhishthira's Downfall:

- He stakes his kingdom, brothers, and finally Draupadi. The law, twisted by Shakuni's cunning, allows it.

- Legal Realist Lens: The game's rules are arbitrary but enforced by the throne's authority. As Llewellyn said: "Law is what officials do."

2. Draupadi's Question:

- "Can a man who has lost himself stake another's freedom?" Her challenge is a legal realist's cry: Why do we obey unjust laws?

- The elders' silence answers her. Bhishma, Drona, and Vidura—custodians of dharma—prioritize loyalty to the throne over justice.

3. Divine Intervention:

- Krishna's miracle (infinite sari) exposes the law's fragility. The courtroom, a hall of "order," collapses into chaos.

Philosophical Threads:

- Holmes' "Bad Man" Theory:

 - "If you want to know the law, ask what the bad man—the one who doesn't care about morality—thinks it is."

 - Duryodhana is Holmes' "bad man." He uses law to humiliate, knowing the elders won't stop him.

- Hart's "Rule of Recognition":

 - Laws are valid if recognized by those in power. The Kauravas' laws are "valid" because the king enforces them.

Questions to the Reader:

1. Is Bhishma's vow to the throne a noble duty or moral cowardice?

2. Can law ever be separated from the people who wield it?

3. If you were Vidura, would you break your silence even if it meant exile or death?

The Elders' Silence as Legal Realism's Triumph:

- Bhishma: Embodies the judge who upholds "procedure" over justice.

- Drona: The scholar who rationalizes oppression ("I owe the throne my loyalty").

- Vidura: The conflicted realist who knows the law is corrupt but fears rebellion.

 "The law, in its majestic equality, forbids the rich and the poor alike to sleep under bridges." – Anatole France (1894).

Historical Parallel: When "Just Following Orders" Became a Crime

In 1945, the world witnessed a legal reckoning. Nazi officers stood trial at Nuremberg for atrocities committed during WWII. Their defense? "We were following the law." Hitler's regime had codified racism, genocide, and conquest into law—legal realism's grotesque zenith. The Allies, however, rejected this, prosecuting Nazis for "crimes against humanity," a term born from natural law's insistence on universal morality.

The Kauravas in Uniform:

- Nazi Judges: Enforced racial purity laws, mirroring the Kauravas' abuse of dharma to justify Draupadi's humiliation.

- Corporate Collaborators: Companies like IG Farben (which produced Zyklon B gas) echoed the elders' complicity—profiting from oppression while hiding behind "legality."

Legal Realism's Dilemma:

The trials posed a searing question: Can law exist without morality? The Nazis' crimes were "legal" under their regime, but the Nuremberg judges declared: "Some laws are too evil to obey." This echoed Draupadi's defiance—a demand that justice transcend power's parchment.

Bridge to Today: The Algorithms of Oppression

- Surveillance States: China's Social Credit System and the NSA's bulk data collection are "legal" yet erode freedom. Like the Kauravas, governments weaponize law to control.

- Corporate Sovereignty: Tech giants like Meta exploit privacy laws to sell user data. Their defense? "We comply with local regulations." This is Duryodhana's gambit—using law to mask exploitation.

Question to the Reader:

When Uber tracks drivers' every move or Amazon busts unions under "contract law," whose "order" are they enforcing—yours or the powerful?

Conclusion: The Unsilencing – What Will You Choose?

The Mahabharata's courtroom never adjourned. It lives in:

- Boardrooms where profit is coded into law.

- Courthouses where bail is denied to the poor but granted to the privileged.

- Your silence when a friend jokes about caste or gender.

Legal realism teaches us: Law is not a shield but a sword—and who wields it matters. The elders' failure was not ignorance but choice. Bhishma chose loyalty, Vidura chose fear, Draupadi chose rebellion.

Final Reflection:

Philosopher Hannah Arendt, reporting on Nazi Adolf Eichmann's trial, coined the term "banality of evil"—the horror of ordinary people enabling atrocity through silence. The Mahabharata whispers: Evil is not just banal; it is bureaucratic. It thrives in the gap between law and justice.

Call to Action:

Next time you hear "It's the law," ask Draupadi's question: "Who owns this law?" Then ask yours:

- Will I be Bhishma—compliant?

- Vidura—silent?

- Or Draupadi—unflinching?

The dice are in your hands.

12. Krishna's Pragmatism – Breaking Rules

Philosophy Unveiled – What is Pragmatism?

Pragmatism is the belief that the value of an idea or action lies in its practical results, not in fixed rules or ideals. It asks: Does this work? rather than Is this right? Born in 19th-century America, pragmatism became a tool to navigate a changing world, blending logic, ethics, and real-world problem-solving.

Key Thinkers and Their Ideas

1. William James (1842–1910):

   James, often called the father of pragmatism, argued that "truth is what works." For example, if believing in free will helps you live a purposeful life, then free will is "true" for you. He famously wrote, "The ultimate test of what a truth means is the conduct it dictates."

2. John Dewey (1859–1952):

   Dewey saw pragmatism as a force for social progress. He believed education should teach critical thinking, not memorization, so people could solve problems like poverty or injustice. To Dewey, democracy itself was a pragmatic experiment—a way to adapt laws to people's needs.

3. Charles Sanders Peirce (1839–1914):

Peirce, who coined the term pragmatism, focused on how ideas clarify confusion. He argued that beliefs are habits—tools we use to act effectively.

Pragmatism in Practice

- Medicine: A doctor might withhold a terminal diagnosis to give a patient hope.

- Politics: A leader might compromise on ideals to pass a law that helps millions.

- Everyday Life: Lying to protect a friend's feelings.

The Debate:

Critics call pragmatism morally slippery. For instance, a government might justify spying on citizens "for safety," eroding privacy. Pragmatists reply: If the action causes harm, it wasn't truly pragmatic. True pragmatism, they argue, requires weighing long-term consequences, not just short-term gains.

Why It Matters Today:

Pragmatism shapes modern ethics. Climate activists, for example, chain themselves to coal plants, breaking laws to force environmental action. Tech companies bypass privacy norms to innovate. The question is: When do ends justify means?

The Unbeatable Bhishma: A Crisis of Duty

The Kurukshetra war was stuck. Bhishma, the grandsire of the Kuru dynasty, stood on the battlefield like a mountain—unshakable, invincible. His boon was cruel: he could only die when he chose to. For nine days, he slaughtered Pandava soldiers, his loyalty to the throne overriding his love for the Pandavas. Arjuna, the greatest archer, froze. How could he raise his bow against a man who taught him to fight?

Krishna's Frustration:

Krishna, Arjuna's charioteer, watched as Bhishma's arrows rained death. "This is not a war of bows," he muttered. "It's a war of dharma." But dharma—the cosmic law—was tangled here. Bhishma's vows bound him to a corrupt throne. The Pandavas' cause was just, but their hands were tied by rules of "honorable war."

The Shikhandi Gambit: Exploiting Loopholes

Krishna devised a plan. Shikhandi, born a woman (Amba) and later reborn as a man, carried a unique power: Bhishma had sworn never to fight a woman. To kill him, Arjuna would attack from behind Shikhandi, using them as a human shield.

The Ethical Storm:

- Arjuna hesitated: "This is deceit! Warriors don't hide behind others!"

- Krishna snapped: "Is your pride worth more than justice? Bhishma uses vows to shield evil. Break the rules, or lose the war."

Reluctantly, Arjuna fired. Bhishma, pierced by arrows, fell. His final words were haunting: "Thank you, Krishna. Only you could free me from my vows."

Questions for the Reader:

- Was Krishna's trickery justified, or did it stain the Pandavas' victory?

- Can "good" people bend rules without losing their morality?

Karna's Downfall: The Cost of "Fair Play"

Later, Karna—the tragic hero born to a charioteer but gifted with divine weapons—entered the fray. His rivalry with Arjuna was personal. During their duel, Karna invoked the Nagastra, a serpent-shaped arrow meant to kill Arjuna. Krishna, foreseeing disaster, pressed his foot into the earth, sinking their chariot. The arrow struck Arjuna's crown instead of his heart.

When Karna's chariot wheel stuck in mud, he begged for time to free it—a rule of honorable combat. Krishna laughed bitterly: "Where was 'fair play' when Draupadi was disrobed? Attack now, Arjuna!" Arjuna fired, ending Karna's life mid-plea.

Karna's death was not noble. He died humiliated, cursing Krishna: "You preach dharma but practice deceit!" Even Arjuna felt guilt. The victory tasted like ash.

Questions for the Reader:

- Did Krishna's pragmatism save the world or corrupt it?

- Is it fair to abandon ethics when your opponent does?

The Cost of Victory

The war ended. The Pandavas won, but their hearts were heavy. Bhishma lay on a bed of arrows for days, teaching Yudhishthira about kingship until his last breath. Karna's sons were slaughtered. Draupadi, who dreamed of justice, ruled a broken kingdom.

Krishna's pragmatism saved the world from Duryodhana's greed, but it left scars. As William James warned: "Ideals must be weighed against their consequences."

The Mahabharata asks us: What price are we willing to pay for victory? Krishna's answer was clear: Break rules, carry guilt, but protect the greater good.

The Manhattan Project: Science, Morality, and the Bomb

In 1942, during World War II, the U.S. launched the Manhattan Project, a secret mission to build the atomic bomb. Scientists like J. Robert Oppenheimer knew the weapon could end the war but would kill thousands. When the first bomb exploded in 1945, Oppenheimer famously quoted the Bhagavad Gita: "Now I am become Death, the destroyer of worlds." Days later, bombs dropped on Hiroshima and Nagasaki killed over 200,000 people, mostly civilians. The war ended, but the world entered the nuclear age—a time of fear and moral reckoning.

Pragmatism in Action

The scientists faced a Krishna-like choice:

- Goal: End the war swiftly, saving millions of lives from prolonged conflict.

- Means: Use a weapon of unimaginable destruction, knowing it would massacre innocents.

President Truman justified the bomb as a "lesser evil," echoing Krishna's logic. Critics called it a war crime. Pragmatists argued: If the bomb saved more lives than it took, was it justified?

Connection to Krishna's Pragmatism

Like Krishna, the Manhattan Project leaders broke ethical rules for a "greater good":

1. Exploiting Loopholes: Just as Krishna used Shikhandi to bypass Bhishma's vow, scientists used nuclear fission—a neutral scientific discovery—for mass destruction.

2. Moral Sacrifices: Krishna accepted guilt for Bhishma's and Karna's deaths; Oppenheimer lived with guilt, calling the bomb a "sin."

3. Unintended Consequences: The Pandavas' victory led to a broken kingdom; the bomb's success sparked a nuclear arms race that still threatens humanity.

Questions for the Reader:

- Was dropping the bomb a necessary evil or an unforgivable act?

- Can science ever be "neutral," or is it always shaped by how we use it?

- Would you make the same choice as Truman or Krishna?

Conclusion: The Tightrope of Pragmatism

Krishna's pragmatism and the Manhattan Project reveal a harsh truth: the world is rarely black and white. Rules matter, but blind obedience to them can perpetuate suffering. Yet bending rules risks normalizing cruelty.

The Mahabharata's Warning

The Pandavas won the war but lost their joy. Arjuna's hands trembled for years; Yudhishthira ruled a haunted kingdom. Krishna's pragmatism saved dharma but left scars. Similarly, the atomic bomb ended WWII but cast a shadow over humanity's future.

Today's Pragmatic Dilemmas

- AI Ethics: Should we slow AI development to prevent misuse, even if it delays life-saving innovations?

- Climate Crisis: Do we prioritize cutting emissions (hurting economies) or adapt reactively (risking disaster)?

- Personal Choices: Is lying to protect a friend's feelings kind or cowardly?

Pragmatism isn't about abandoning ethics—it's about weighing consequences in an imperfect world. Krishna taught that duty (karma) must be detached from personal gain. But he also warned: "To hesitate in the face of evil is the greatest sin."

Ask yourself:

- Where is my line between "necessary evil" and "unacceptable compromise"?

- Can I act decisively, like Krishna or Oppenheimer, and still sleep at night?

The Mahabharata doesn't give easy answers. It asks us to walk the tightrope—eyes open, heart heavy, striving to balance ideals with the messy reality of survival.

13. Karna's Despair & Nihilism

Philosophy Unveiled – What is Nihilism?

Nihilism is the belief that life lacks inherent meaning, purpose, or value. It suggests that traditional morals, goals, and truths are human inventions, not divine or universal. Think of it as staring into an abyss and realizing the abyss stares back—emptily.

 Key Thinkers and Their Shadows

1. Friedrich Nietzsche (1844–1900):

  Nietzsche famously declared "God is dead," arguing that society's collapse of religious faith left a void of meaning. But he didn't celebrate nihilism; he warned against it. For him, the Übermensch (Overman) must create meaning in a meaningless world. Yet, Karna's cry—"I am nothing"—reflects the despair of those who fail to rise.

2. Albert Camus (1913–1960):

  Camus saw life as absurd: humans crave meaning, but the universe offers none. His essay The Myth of

Sisyphus asks: Do we succumb to despair or rebel? Karna's life mirrors Sisyphus—pushing the boulder of honor up a hill, only to watch it roll down.

3. Arthur Schopenhauer (1788–1860):

Schopenhauer viewed existence as perpetual suffering. His nihilism was passive: "Life is a business that does not cover the costs."

Nihilism in Practice

- Religion: If there's no divine plan, rituals and prayers are empty.

- Morality: If life has no purpose, why be kind or just?

- Identity: If society's labels (caste, race, gender) are illusions, who are we?

The Debate:

Nietzsche urged us to "become who you are" beyond societal norms. But what if society crushes that chance? Karna's struggle—born a prince but rejected as a charioteer's son—exposes nihilism's danger: when the world denies you meaning, you become nothing.

Tragic Hero: Born to Lose

Karna's life began with abandonment. Kunti, his mother, floated him down a river to hide her shame. Found by a charioteer, he grew up as "low-born" in a caste-obsessed world. Yet, he burned with greatness. He mastered archery in secret, matching Arjuna's skill. But when he sought recognition at a royal tournament, the Pandavas mocked him: "A charioteer's son cannot compete with princes." Duryodhana, the Kaurava prince, crowned him King of Anga—not out of respect, but to spite the Pandavas.

Nietzsche's Lens:

Karna's ambition mirrors the will to power—the drive to transcend limits. But society's walls (caste, fate) crushed him. Nietzsche wrote: "He who has a why to live can bear almost any how." Karna's why—proving his worth—was a flame the world smothered.

The Curse of Invisible Chains

Karna's suffering deepened with curses:

- Guru Parashurama cursed him to forget his skills in battle when he lied about his caste to learn archery.

- A Brahmin cursed him for accidentally killing his cow, ensuring his chariot wheel would trap him during his final fight.

Each curse reinforced his nihilism: No matter how hard he fought, fate conspired to erase him.

Camus' Absurdity:

Like Sisyphus, Karna woke each day to push against cosmic indifference. His loyalty to Duryodhana—a tyrant—wasn't love but a cry: "If I cannot be remembered as a hero, let me be remembered as loyal."

The Battlefield: A Theatre of Nothingness

On Kurukshetra's plains, Karna faced Arjuna. Krishna, Arjuna's charioteer, exposed Karna's birth secret mid-duel: "You are Kunti's son! A Pandava! Stop this fratricide!" For a moment, hope flickered. But Karna snarled: "You offer me family now, when I've lived as a beggar? I choose loyalty over blood."

Schopenhauer's Shadow:

Karna's choice reflects nihilistic futility. He clung to Duryodhana—the man who used him—because meaninglessness is less terrifying than irrelevance.

When his chariot wheel sank into the earth (the Brahmin's curse), he begged Arjuna to pause—a warrior's code. Krishna laughed: "Where was this code when Draupadi wept?" Arjuna fired. Karna died as he lived: unseen, unloved, a footnote in someone else's epic.

Questions for the Reader:

- Can loyalty give life meaning, even if it's misplaced?

- Is Karna a hero (defying fate) or a fool (serving tyrants)?

- Would knowing his birth earlier have saved him, or was his doom inevitable?

Karna's sons were slaughtered. His wife mourned alone. Even his golden armor—the symbol of his divine birth—was stripped away. In death, he became a cautionary tale: "Pride goes before destruction." But Nietzsche might argue: "He was destroyed not by pride, but a world that refused to see him."

Philosophical Threads

- Nietzsche's Übermensch vs. Caste: Karna's potential was suffocated by societal hierarchies. Can one self-create in a rigged system?

- Camus' Rebellion: Karna's life was absurd. His rebellion—choosing loyalty—was his "scorn of the gods."

- Schopenhauer's Pessimism: His death mirrors Schopenhauer's view: "Life is a losing game."

Bridge to Today

Karna's cry—"I am nothing"—resonates in modern despair:

- Identity Crises: Social media's illusion of validation.

- Systemic Oppression: Marginalized communities fighting erasure.

- Existential Burnout: Millennials dubbed the "why bother?" generation.

Final Reflection:

Nihilism isn't surrender; it's the first step to choosing meaning. Karna failed, but his tragedy asks us: What will we create in the void?

Modern Parallel: The Artist Who Lived in the Shadows

Vincent van Gogh, one of history's most celebrated painters, died believing he was a failure. In his lifetime, he sold just one painting, battled mental illness, and was shunned by society. He wrote to his brother Theo: "What am I in the eyes of most people? A nonentity, an eccentric, or an unpleasant person. Someone who has no position in society and never will have." Like Karna, van Gogh's genius was dismissed because he didn't fit societal norms—a poor, mentally ill outsider in a world obsessed with status and stability.

Nihilism in Color:

Van Gogh's The Starry Night—a swirling sky over a sleepy village—captures the tension between cosmic awe and human insignificance. His bold strokes scream: "Does my existence matter?" Yet, he painted furiously, creating over 2,000 works, as if art could fill the void. Nietzsche might call this "will to power"— creating meaning where none exists. But for van Gogh, it was a losing battle. He died by suicide at 37, unknown and broke.

Connection to Karna's Tragedy

- Rejection by Society:

Karna was mocked as a "charioteer's son"; van Gogh was called a "madman." Both were denied dignity because of labels.

- Loyalty to a Flawed Cause:

Karna clung to Duryodhana, who exploited him. Van Gogh clung to art, which society ignored.

- Posthumous Redemption:

Karna became a tragic hero in retellings; van Gogh's paintings now sell for millions. But what comfort is fame to the dead?

Camus' Absurd Rebellion:

Van Gogh's relentless painting, despite despair, mirrors Camus' Sisyphus: "One must imagine Sisyphus happy." Each brushstroke was rebellion against meaninglessness. Karna's loyalty to Duryodhana was his rebellion—a choice to be someone, even if that someone was a pawn.

Questions for the Reader:

- Can creating art (or loyalty) justify a life of suffering?

- Is posthumous fame a triumph—or proof of life's cruelty?

Conclusion: Finding Light in the Abyss

Karna and van Gogh teach us that nihilism isn't the end—it's a crossroads. Their lives force us to ask: When the world denies you meaning, do you surrender, or do you create your own?

Modern Echoes of Despair :

- Social Media and Identity: Teens curate perfect online personas while feeling "nothing" inside— Karna's cry in a digital age.

- Systemic Erasure: Marginalized communities (Dalits, LGBTQ+, refugees) fighting to be seen in societies that dismiss them.

- Burnout Culture: Millennials grinding in jobs that offer no purpose—a mundane nihilism.

Nietzsche's Challenge

Nietzsche urged us to "become who you are" beyond society's scripts. For Karna, that meant rejecting his birth secret and owning his loyalty. For van Gogh, it meant painting skies that screamed his turmoil. For us, it might mean:

- Rejecting toxic hustle culture to find work that matters.

- Embracing flaws as part of our story, not shame.

- Creating meaning through small acts: art, kindness, rebellion.

Final Questions:

- What societal "labels" make you feel like "nothing"? How can you redefine them?

- If life has no built-in purpose, what will you build anyway?

- Is your rebellion against the void loud (like van Gogh's art) or quiet (like Karna's loyalty)?

14. Bhima's Rage & Virtue Ethics

Philosophy Unveiled – What is Virtue Ethics?

Virtue Ethics is a philosophy that focuses on character over rules or outcomes. It asks: What kind of person should I be? rather than What should I do? Rooted in ancient Greek thought, it teaches that moral excellence (virtue) lies in balancing emotions and actions—neither too much nor too little.

Aristotle and the Golden Mean

Aristotle (384–322 BCE), the father of Virtue Ethics, argued that every virtue is a midpoint between two extremes:

- Courage: Between cowardice (too little bravery) and recklessness (too much).

- Generosity: Between stinginess and wastefulness.

- Anger: Between apathy (too little concern) and rage (uncontrolled fury).

For Aristotle, virtues are habits cultivated through practice. A virtuous person isn't born good—they become good by repeatedly choosing balance.

Example: A student facing bullying.

- Cowardice: Staying silent.

- Recklessness: Starting a physical fight.

- Courage: Confronting the bully calmly or seeking help.

Modern Virtue Ethicists

- Alasdair MacIntyre: Revived Virtue Ethics in the 20th century, arguing modern society has lost "moral compasses." He praised traditions (like the Mahabharata) that teach virtue through storytelling.

- Martha Nussbaum: Linked virtues to empathy, urging us to see the world through others' eyes.

Debate: Critics argue virtues are vague. What's "balanced" in one culture (e.g., assertiveness) might be rude in another. Aristotle replied: Virtue is learned through community and context.

Why It Matters Today:

In polarized times, Virtue Ethics teaches us to avoid extremes:

- Social Media: Between mindless scrolling (apathy) and online rage (toxicity).

- Activism: Between silence and violence.

Bhima: The Pandava of Unbridled Fury

Bhima, second eldest of the Pandavas, was a mountain of muscle and temper. His laughter shook palaces; his rage reduced enemies to ash. But beneath his brute strength lay a heart loyal to his family and dharma.

Key Moments of Virtue and Excess:

1. The Lacquer House Plot:

  The Kauravas tried to burn the Pandavas alive in a wax palace. Bhima, known for his appetite, carried his family to safety—a mix of strength (virtue) and impulsiveness (he nearly attacked the Kauravas, risking exposure).

2. Draupadi's Humiliation:

When Draupadi was disrobed in court, Bhima's vow to kill Dushasana and drink his blood was both heroic (loyalty) and extreme (bloodlust).

3. The Slaying of Dushasana:

Bhima tore open Dushasana's chest, fulfilling his vow. Was this justice or vengeance?

Aristotle's Lens: Bhima's Struggle for the Golden Mean

- Strength as Virtue: Bhima's power protected his family (e.g., defeating demons like Bakasura).

- Rage as Excess: His fury often blinded him (e.g., killing Kauravas brutally, ignoring Yudhishthira's pleas for restraint).

Aristotle's Question: Can virtue exist without self-control?

Bhima's loyalty was virtuous, but his anger tipped into vice. Even Krishna warned him: "Unchecked fire destroys the arsonist."

The Complexity of Righteous Anger

Bhima's rage wasn't mindless. It was a response to grave injustice:

- The Pandavas' exile.

- Draupadi's assault.

- The theft of their kingdom.

Questions for the Reader:

1. Can extreme actions ever be virtuous in an unjust world?

2. Is Bhima a hero or a cautionary tale?

3. When has your anger helped—or harmed—your cause?

The Aftermath: Bhima's Redemption

After the war, Bhima ruled with surprising wisdom. He tempered his rage, showing growth. Yet, he never regretted killing Dushasana. To him, it was necessary excess—a flaw that served dharma.

Aristotle's Verdict:

Virtue requires lifelong practice. Bhima's journey—from hotheaded warrior to measured king—mirrors Aristotle's belief that "we are what we repeatedly do."

Rosa Parks and the Power of Balanced Resistance

In 1955, Rosa Parks refused to give up her bus seat to a white passenger in Montgomery, Alabama. Her act of defiance was neither passive nor violent—it was a calculated stance against injustice. The subsequent Montgomery Bus Boycott, led by Dr. Martin Luther King Jr., lasted 381 days. Protesters walked miles to work, carpooled, and faced arrests, yet they adhered to nonviolent resistance. This strategy mirrored Aristotle's Golden Mean: rejecting both submission (cowardice) and violent retaliation (recklessness) in favor of disciplined courage.

Aristotle's Lens:

- Cowardice: Accepting segregation silently.

- Recklessness: Riots or armed retaliation.

- Courage: Organized, nonviolent protest.

Dr. King called this "soul force"—a virtue born of restraint and moral clarity. Like Bhima protecting

Draupadi, the boycotters channeled rage into purposeful action.

Bhima's Rage vs. Civil Rights Strategy

Bhima's vow to kill Dushasana was visceral, but the Civil Rights Movement showed how anger could be harnessed, not suppressed. Protesters faced police dogs, fire hoses, and beatings without retaliation. Their discipline was not weakness—it was strategic virtue.

Parallels:

- Bhima's Oath: A promise to destroy evil (Dushasana's insult to Draupadi).

- MLK's Oath: "We will wear them down by our capacity to suffer."

Both transformed raw emotion into a weapon of dharma or justice.

Questions for the Reader:

- Is nonviolence always the "right" choice, or are some evils too great to endure?

- Can anger ever be a virtue, or must it always be tempered?

Conclusion: The Tightrope of Virtue – Lessons from Bhima and Montgomery

Bhima's story and the Civil Rights Movement reveal anger's duality:

- Destructive: Unchecked rage destroys trust and humanity (Bhima's bloodlust, violent riots).

- Constructive: Focused anger fuels justice (Bhima protecting his family, sit-ins desegregating lunch counters).

Aristotle's Golden Mean isn't about eliminating emotion but directing it. As Martha Nussbaum wrote: "Anger, when rightly ordered, is a sign that we care about what is just."

Today's world demands similar balance:

- Social Media Outrage: Between apathy (scrolling past injustice) and "cancel culture" (destroying lives over mistakes).

- Workplace Conflicts: Between silence (enduring harassment) and explosive confrontations (burning bridges).

- Personal Relationships: Between swallowing hurt (resentment) and lashing out (damaging bonds).

Bhima's Redemption:

By the war's end, Bhima learned to temper his fury. He ruled wisely, showing that virtue is a journey, not a fixed trait. Similarly, Dr. King's movement emphasized redemptive love—a commitment to justice without dehumanizing opponents.

Final Reflection

Aristotle asked: "What is the right feeling, toward the right person, to the right degree, at the right time?" Bhima and Rosa Parks answer: Virtue is knowing when to roar and when to breathe.

Ask yourself:

1. When has your anger served a purpose? When has it harmed?

2. What "golden mean" do you struggle to find (e.g., confidence vs. arrogance, honesty vs. cruelty)?

3. Can you channel your rage into a force for good, or does it control you?

"The ultimate measure of a person is not where they stand in moments of comfort, but where they stand in times of challenge." – Martin Luther King Jr.

15. Shakuni's Revenge & Ethical Egoism

Philosophy Unveiled – What is Ethical Egoism?

Ethical Egoism is the belief that individuals should act in their own self-interest, and that doing so is not just practical but morally right. Unlike selfishness, which ignores others' needs, ethical egoism argues that prioritizing oneself can lead to better outcomes for everyone. Imagine a doctor who works hard to become wealthy—this ambition drives them to save lives skillfully. Their success benefits both themselves and their patients.

Key Thinkers and Ideas

1. Ayn Rand (1905–1982):

The philosopher-novelist championed Objectivism, a philosophy celebrating rational self-interest. She wrote, "The virtue of selfishness is the pursuit of one's own happiness." For Rand, sacrificing for others is immoral if it denies your own worth.

2. Max Stirner (1806–1856):

Stirner's "The Ego and Its Own" declared that individuals should reject societal norms and act solely for themselves. He saw morality as a tool to control people.

Core Idea:

Ethical egoists don't say, "Crush others to win." They argue that enlightened self-interest—like honesty in business or kindness to build trust—creates a thriving society.

Debate:

Critics ask: What if my self-interest harms others? For example, a CEO cutting jobs to boost profits. Ethical egoists reply: True self-interest avoids harming others, as conflict often backfires. But is this realistic?

The Humiliation of Gandhari

Shakuni, prince of Gandhara, watched his sister Gandhari marry Dhritarashtra, the blind king of Hastinapura. To "equalize" her life with her husband's blindness, Gandhari blindfolded herself forever. The Kurus mocked this sacrifice, treating her as a pawn in their politics. Shakuni's rage festered: "They reduced my sister to a symbol, not a person."

Shakuni swore to destroy the Kuru dynasty. His weapon? A game of dice.

- The Trap: He crafted loaded dice from his father's bones, symbolizing his singular focus on revenge.

- The Stakes: He manipulated Yudhishthira, the eldest Pandava, into gambling his kingdom, brothers, and wife Draupadi.

Ethical Egoism in Action:

Shakuni's actions were coldly rational:

1. Self-Preservation: He survived in a hostile court by appearing harmless.

2. Strategic Patience: He waited years to strike, ensuring his plan was flawless.

3. Maximizing Gain: His revenge wasn't impulsive—it aimed to erase the Kurus' legacy.

But was this enlightened self-interest? His scheme caused mass suffering: the Pandavas' exile, Draupadi's humiliation, and a catastrophic war.

Questions for the Reader:

- Is Shakuni's revenge justified if it avenges his sister's dignity?

- Can self-interest ever align with morality when it harms others?

- Would Ayn Rand praise Shakuni's cunning or condemn his destructiveness?

The Aftermath: Pyrrhic Victory

Shakuni died in the Kurukshetra war, his revenge complete but his soul empty. His self-interest saved no one—not Gandhari, not himself. The Mahabharata asks: When does ambition become a cage?

Philosophical Threads

- Rand's Objectivism vs. Shakuni's Nihilism: Rand believed self-interest required reason and respect for others' rights. Shakuni's actions, though calculated, ignored this balance.

- Stirner's Rebellion: Shakuni rejected societal duty, much like Stirner's "egoist," but his vengeance consumed him.

The Collapse of Lehman Brothers: Self-Interest Gone Rogue

In 2008, the world watched as the U.S. housing market collapsed, triggering a global financial crisis. Banks like Lehman Brothers had prioritized short-term profits over long-term stability, approving risky subprime mortgages to unqualified borrowers. Traders bundled these toxic loans into complex financial products, sold them as "safe" investments, and reaped massive bonuses. Their mantra? "If it makes money, it's justified."

Ethical Egoism in Action:

- Self-Interest: Bankers chased bonuses and promotions, believing their success would trickle down.

- Ignored Harm: Millions lost homes, jobs, and savings. The crisis exposed how unchecked self-interest—devoid of ethics—destroys trust and stability.

Ayn Rand's Blind Spot:

Rand argued rational self-interest benefits society. But the 2008 crisis revealed a flaw: when individuals define "rational" as "what enriches me now," they ignore systemic consequences. Shakuni's dice game mirrors this—his revenge helped him "win," but it burned down the very world he sought to rule.

Shakuni's Shadow in Wall Street's Greed

Shakuni's revenge and the 2008 crisis share a dark thread: the illusion of control.

- Shakuni: Used loaded dice to manipulate the Kauravas and Pandavas, believing he could outsmart fate.

- Bankers: Used complex financial instruments to mask risk, believing they could outsmart the market.

Both failed to see their actions as part of a larger web. Shakuni's war erased his family's legacy; the bankers' greed eroded public trust in capitalism.

Questions for the Reader:

- Can self-interest ever be "ethical" if it ignores collateral damage?

- When does ambition become a danger to others?

Conclusion: The Tightrope of Self-Interest

1. Self-Interest Needs Boundaries: Shakuni's revenge and reckless banking show that unchecked ambition corrupts. Ethical egoism works only when aligned with empathy and foresight.

2. The Myth of Isolation: No one acts in a vacuum. Shakuni's schemes destroyed his family; bankers' bets crashed the global economy.

The epic ends with Shakuni dead, the Kurus annihilated, and the Pandavas ruling a wasteland. Victory, built on selfishness, leaves everyone hollow.

Ask Yourself:

- Have I ever pursued a goal so fiercely that I harmed others? Did the end justify the means?

- How can I balance my ambitions with responsibility to others?

Final Reflection

Ethical egoism isn't inherently evil—it's human. But as Krishna tells Arjuna: "The wise see themselves in all beings." Shakuni and the bankers forgot this. Their stories urge us to ask: Will your self-interest lift others or bury them?

A Choice:

- Shakuni's Path: Burn the world to warm yourself.

- Krishna's Path: Act with courage and compassion.

The Mahabharata doesn't judge—it invites us to choose.

16. War's Aftermath & Postmodern Relativism

Postmodern relativism emerges as a philosophical response to the idea of absolute truths, arguing that meaning, morality, and reality are not fixed but shaped by cultural, historical, and individual perspectives. Unlike classical philosophies that seek universal principles—Plato's Forms or Kant's categorical imperative—postmodernism dissolves grand narratives into a mosaic of subjective experiences. Michel Foucault, a key figure, claimed that power structures dictate what societies accept as "true," embedding authority in institutions like governments, schools, and media. For instance, colonial histories written by conquerors often erase indigenous voices, illustrating how truth is a construct of dominance rather than an immutable fact. Jacques Derrida's deconstruction further unravels binaries like good/evil or victor/vanquished, revealing their instability. A courtroom verdict, for example, might be "just" in legal terms but feel oppressive to marginalized communities, exposing the fluidity of justice. Jean-François Lyotard dismissed grand narratives like progress or enlightenment as myths, urging skepticism toward claims of universal morality. This skepticism resonates in modern debates: Is democracy inherently "good," or does its value depend on cultural context? Postmodernism doesn't deny truth but insists it is plural—a chorus of voices, not a solo.

The Mahabharata Story – Ashwatthama's Curse and the Weight of Ambiguity

The Kurukshetra war ends not with triumph but exhaustion. The Pandavas stand victorious, yet their kingdom lies in ashes, their kin slaughtered, their consciences heavy with moral compromises. The war's aftermath is a landscape of unresolved questions, where even justice feels like a shifting mirage. Consider Ashwatthama, the warrior who massacres Pandava heirs in their sleep to avenge his father's death. When Krishna curses him to wander the earth, immortal but tormented, the punishment defies easy judgment. Is Ashwatthama a villain or a tragic son? The epic refuses to say. His curse embodies postmodern relativism: suffering without redemption, justice without clarity.

The Pandavas themselves grapple with fractured truths. Yudhishthira, the "righteous" king, ascends the throne only to drown in guilt. His adherence to dharma during the war—lying to kill Drona, sanctioning Bhima's brutality—haunts him. When he questions whether his victories were morally justified, the text offers no solace. Even Krishna, the divine strategist, avoids absolutes. His cosmic perspective in the Bhagavad Gita ("I am Time, the destroyer") clashes with the human need for moral certainty. The war's ethical chaos mirrors Derrida's deconstruction: the line between duty and sin blurs, and every "truth" unravels under scrutiny.

The elders, too, dissect the war's legacy in contradictory ways. Bhishma, on his bed of arrows, lectures Yudhishthira on kingship but dies before resolving his own complicity in Draupadi's humiliation. Vidura, the wise minister, condemns the Kauravas' greed but never absolves the Pandavas' ruthlessness. These voices, layered and conflicted, reflect Foucault's assertion that knowledge is never neutral—it is a battleground of competing interests.

In the final books, the Pandavas renounce the throne and walk into the Himalayas, seeking absolution. Yet their departure feels less like resolution than surrender. The epic closes not with answers but with a void—a recognition that some truths are too fractured to reconcile. Postmodernism's shadow looms here: the refusal to crown a single narrative as supreme. The Mahabharata becomes a mirror, asking us to sit with discomfort, to accept that morality, like history, is a story told by the survivors, riddled with omissions and biases.

Questions for Reflection:

- Can a "just war" exist if its aftermath breeds endless suffering?

- Is Ashwatthama's curse fair, or does it perpetuate the cycle of violence it seeks to condemn?

- How do we judge the Pandavas' actions when their victories are stained by deceit?

The Mahabharata, like postmodernism, offers no verdicts—only the uneasy task of navigating a world where truths are many, and certainty is a myth.

Modern Parallel – The Vietnam War and the Fractured Narratives of Truth

The Vietnam War, like the Mahabharata's Kurukshetra, left a legacy steeped in contradiction and contested truths. For the U.S. government, the war was framed as a noble fight against communism, a "domino theory" imperative to save Southeast Asia.

For Vietnamese revolutionaries, it was a struggle for independence against colonial oppression. Civilians caught in the crossfire, however, experienced it as an unending nightmare of burned villages, Agent Orange, and shattered families. The My Lai Massacre of 1968 epitomizes this clash of narratives: U.S. soldiers slaughtered over 500 unarmed Vietnamese civilians, an event initially covered up as a "victory" before whistleblowers exposed the atrocity. Decades later, American textbooks still debate whether the massacre was an isolated tragedy or a symptom of systemic dehumanization, while Vietnamese memorials honor the dead as martyrs of resistance.

This fragmentation mirrors the Mahabharata's refusal to crown a single truth. Just as Ashwatthama's curse defies moral categorization—punishing a war crime with eternal suffering—the Vietnam War resists simplistic judgment. Was the U.S. soldier who followed orders a villain or a victim? Was the Viet Cong fighter a terrorist or a freedom fighter? Postmodern thinkers like Foucault would argue that power structures shape these labels: the victors write history, but the vanquished preserve counter-narratives in art, oral traditions, and protest. The iconic Vietnam Veterans Memorial in Washington, with its stark list of names, and Trần Văn Cẩn's paintings of wartime horror, together form a mosaic of truths, each valid yet incomplete.

Conclusion: Living in the Gray – The Postmodern Imperative

The Mahabharata and the Vietnam War teach us that moral clarity is often an illusion. Postmodern relativism does not deny truth but insists it is multifaceted—a prism rather than a monolith. Ashwatthama's curse, the Pandavas' hollow victory, and the My Lai Massacre all reject the comfort of binaries. They force us to ask: Can we condemn without understanding? Can we heal without absolving?

In today's world, where social media amplifies competing narratives and political rhetoric reduces complexity to slogans, postmodernism offers a vital tool: the humility to listen. It urges us to question whose truths are amplified and whose are silenced. When we encounter a "terrorist" or a "hero," a "criminal" or a "victim," we might pause to ask: What stories are missing? What power dynamics shape this label?

The Mahabharata ends with the Pandavas walking into the Himalayas, seeking peace not in answers but in release from the burden of judgment. Similarly, postmodernism does not resolve contradictions—it invites us to hold them. To live in the gray is not to abandon ethics but to engage more deeply, recognizing that truth, like justice, is a collective work in progress.

Final Reflection:

- Whose narratives dominate your understanding of history? Whose are erased?

- Can empathy coexist with accountability in a world of fragmented truths?

In the end, the Mahabharata and postmodernism alike remind us: certainty is a crutch. Wisdom lies in walking the uncertain path, one fractured truth at a time.

17. The War Itself & Hegelian Dialectics

Philosophy Unveiled – Hegel's Dance of Contradictions

Georg Wilhelm Friedrich Hegel, the 19th-century German philosopher, saw history as a spiral of conflict and resolution. His theory of dialectics argues that progress emerges from the clash of opposing forces: a thesis (an existing idea or system) collides with its antithesis (a counter-idea), leading to a synthesis (a new, higher-order truth). This synthesis then becomes the new thesis, sparking fresh contradictions.

For example, feudalism (thesis) clashed with Enlightenment ideals of liberty (antithesis), birthing modern democracies (synthesis). Hegel believed this process was inevitable and purposeful—a "cunning of reason" where even destructive conflicts serve humanity's evolution. The Mahabharata's war mirrors this idea: the Pandavas and Kauravas, locked in opposition, force a reckoning that reshapes society.

The Mahabharata Story – The War as Cosmic Dialectic

The Kurukshetra battlefield is Hegel's dialectic made flesh. The Pandavas, champions of dharma (thesis), confront the Kauravas, embodiments of adharma (antithesis). Yet both sides are flawed. The Pandavas use deceit to win—Krishna's pragmatism tarnishes their virtue. The Kauravas, though greedy, include noble warriors like Bhishma, bound by oaths to a corrupt throne.

The war's brutality strips away illusions. Bhishma, the grandsire, represents the old order's rigidity—his vows uphold a system that enables Duryodhana's tyranny. His fall on a bed of arrows signals the collapse of blind duty (thesis). Duryodhana's greed (antithesis) is equally unsustainable. His refusal to share power ignites a fire that consumes everything.

From this carnage emerges a fragile synthesis: Yudhishthira's kingship. He rules with remorse, not triumph, enacting laws to uplift the oppressed. The war's trauma forces a new moral awareness—justice must balance duty and compassion. Yet Hegel's spiral continues: Yudhishthira's rule is imperfect, haunted by guilt, foreshadowing future conflicts.

Key Battles as Dialectical Moments

1. Bhishma's Fall: The patriarch's defeat by Shikhandi (a warrior born female) shatters gender and caste norms, challenging the thesis of rigid hierarchy.

2. Karna's Betrayal: The tragic hero, torn between loyalty and birthright, embodies the antithesis of identity—can destiny override societal labels?

3. Draupadi's Silence: After the war, her unspoken trauma becomes a synthesis, forcing the victors to confront the cost of "righteous" violence.

Each battle is a thesis-antithesis collision. Arjuna's internal conflict in the Bhagavad Gita—duty vs. conscience—mirrors Hegel's dialectic within the self. Krishna's counsel ("Act without attachment") reframes synthesis as detachment from outcomes, a transcendence of dualities.

Questions for Reflection :

- Can destruction truly birth a "better" world, or is this a rationalization of violence?

- Is Yudhishthira's remorse a sign of progress or proof that synthesis is always incomplete?

- How do modern conflicts—political, social, personal—reflect Hegel's pattern of clash and resolution?

The Aftermath – A World Forever Changed

The war ends not with triumph but exhaustion. Cities lie ruined, families shattered, and the survivors carry scars no crown can heal. Yet Hegel's "cunning of reason" lingers: the Mahabharata's synthesis is not a utopia but a reckoning. The old order dies, but the new one is born in humility.

Yudhishthira's first act as king is a horse sacrifice—not to celebrate victory, but to atone. This ritual, steeped in ambiguity, acknowledges the dialectic's cost: progress demands sacrifice, but the ledger of suffering never balances. The epic closes with the Pandavas' final journey into the Himalayas, a renunciation of power that questions whether synthesis is an endpoint or another thesis in disguise.

Modern Parallel – The Cold War and the Dialectic of Ideologies

The Cold War (1947–1991) stands as Hegel's dialectic writ large on the global stage. The capitalist West, led by the United States (thesis), clashed with the communist East, spearheaded by the Soviet Union (antithesis). Their ideological rivalry—rooted in opposing visions of freedom, equality, and power— ignited proxy wars, espionage, and a nuclear arms race. Yet this conflict birthed a paradoxical synthesis: globalization. The fall of the Berlin Wall in 1989 symbolized not just the collapse of communism but the emergence of a hybrid world order where capitalist markets absorbed socialist welfare ideals, and democracies coexisted with authoritarian capitalism.

Like the Mahabharata's war, the Cold War revealed the fragility of binaries. The U.S. championed democracy while supporting dictatorships in Chile or Iran. The USSR preached workers' rights while stifling dissent in Hungary or Czechoslovakia. Both sides weaponized morality, mirroring the Pandavas and Kauravas' claim to righteousness. The Cuban Missile Crisis (1962), where the world teetered on nuclear annihilation, echoes the Bhagavad Gita's moment of existential paralysis: Arjuna's despair and Kennedy's diary entry ("I am not altogether sure we're rational") both grapple with the cost of ideological purity.

The synthesis—globalization—is fraught with contradictions. It lifted billions from poverty but entrenched inequality. It connected cultures but eroded traditions. Hegel's "cunning of reason" is evident here: progress is messy, nonlinear, and often blind to human suffering. The Mahabharata's

Yudhishthira, ruling a broken kingdom, mirrors post-Cold War leaders navigating a world where old enemies (Russia, China) resurface as new threats, and ideals (democracy, human rights) buckle under corporate power and populism.

Conclusion: The Spiral Never Ends – Dialectics in Our Time

The Mahabharata and the Cold War teach us that synthesis is not an endpoint but a new thesis awaiting its antithesis. Today's clashes—climate activism vs. corporate greed, AI ethics vs. technological imperialism, nationalism vs. globalism—are fresh iterations of Hegel's dance. The Pandavas' victory, like the Cold War's end, did not usher in utopia but a reckoning with imperfection.

Hegel believed history's dialectic moves toward freedom, but freedom itself is a contested ideal. For Arjuna, it meant fulfilling his duty as a warrior; for a modern protester, it might mean dismantling systems of oppression. The Mahabharata's true lesson is that conflict is inevitable, but how we engage it defines progress. Yudhishthira's remorse, Ashwatthama's curse, and the fallout of Chernobyl all whisper: victory is empty without ethical reflection.

Final Reflection:

- Can we disentangle "progress" from violence, or is struggle inherent to growth?

- What contradictions define your life? How might they spark a personal "synthesis"?

- Is the world's current polarization a necessary dialectic or a failure of imagination?

The Mahabharata ends with the Pandavas walking away from power, seeking peace beyond the dialectic. Yet Hegel's spiral continues. Our task is not to escape conflict but to navigate it with the humility of Yudhishthira and the clarity of Krishna—to fight, not for conquest, but for a synthesis that honors the humanity in all sides.

18. Yudhishthira's Final Test

The Ascent: A Journey Through Unanswered Questions

The Himalayas rise like frozen gods, their peaks slicing through clouds as Yudhishthira, the eldest Pandava, climbs toward heaven. His body is a shadow of its former self—bones brittle, skin clinging to memories of war. Behind him, his brothers and Draupadi have fallen, one by one, victims of a pilgrimage that feels less like redemption and more like a cosmic joke. Only a stray dog trails him now, its matted fur and limping gait a mirror of Yudhishthira's unraveling soul. The air thins. The path vanishes. A voice booms: "Enter heaven, O King. But leave the dog behind."

Yudhishthira pauses. The dog, nameless and loyal, stares up with eyes that hold no judgment, only trust. To abandon it would betray the last shred of his fractured dharma. To refuse would defy the gods. This moment—a collision of duty and absurdity—is the Mahabharata's final test. Not of virtue, but of faith in the unknown.

The Abyss of Divine Logic: Kierkegaard's Absurd

Søren Kierkegaard, the 19th-century Danish philosopher, wrote of the "leap of faith"—a surrender to truths beyond reason, where logic drowns and the soul floats. For him, faith was not a reward for virtue but a rebellion against the absurd. Abraham, ordered to sacrifice his son Isaac, became Kierkegaard's archetype: a man who trusted God's madness without demanding sense.

Yudhishthira stands at a similar precipice. The gods demand he abandon the dog to enter heaven—a command that mocks his lifelong adherence to dharma. But what is dharma here? The rules of kingship? The whims of deities? Or the silent bond between a broken man and a creature that has outlasted empires? Kierkegaard would call this a teleological suspension of the ethical: the moment ethics bows to a higher, unfathomable purpose. Yudhishthira's choice is not between right and wrong, but between the map of morality and the uncharted wilderness of faith.

The Dog as Mirror: A Hindu Camus

The dog is no ordinary animal. In Hindu cosmology, dogs are liminal beings—guides to the underworld, companions of Bhairava (the god of dissolution), symbols of the unclaimed, the unclean, the unresolved. To the gods, it is a test. To Yudhishthira, it is the only truth he has left: loyalty without condition.

Albert Camus, the absurdist philosopher, argued that life's meaning emerges not from answers but from relentless questioning. Sisyphus, condemned to eternally roll a boulder uphill, finds freedom in accepting the futility of his task. Yudhishthira, like Sisyphus, is asked to embrace contradiction: How can heaven, the realm of perfect justice, demand injustice? The dog, silent and persistent, becomes his boulder. To refuse heaven is not despair—it is revolt.

The Illusion of Reward: A Divine Trap

Heaven, in the Mahabharata, is not a paradise but a hall of mirrors. When Yudhishthira finally enters, he finds his enemies blissful and his kin in torment. The gods smirk: "This is a test within a test." The Kauravas, who sowed chaos, enjoy bliss because they never pretended to virtue. The Pandavas, who clung to dharma, are punished for their moral compromises. The message is clear: divine justice is not moral justice. It is a game, absurd and unapologetic.

Kierkegaard's Abraham was rewarded for his blind faith—Isaac spared, legacy secured. Yudhishthira is rewarded with a deeper paradox: heaven's cruelty reveals that virtue, in the end, is a performance. The true test was never about earning heaven but seeing through it.

The Unanswerable Why: Nietzsche's Eternal Return

Friedrich Nietzsche's "eternal recurrence" asks: What if you had to relive your life, every joy and sorrow, endlessly? Would you despair or dance? Yudhishthira's journey mirrors this. His life—a tapestry of war, betrayal, and hollow victories—is a cycle he cannot escape. Even in heaven, the cycle continues: joy is artifice, suffering is revelation.

The dog, revealed as Dharma in disguise, offers no answers. It simply is—a reminder that truth wears the guise of the unwanted, the ignored, the limping. To accept this is to embrace what Nietzsche called amor fati: love of fate. Not because it is fair, but because it is yours.

The Whisper of the Dog: Faith Beyond Gods

In the end, Yudhishthira's refusal to abandon the dog is not piety but a rejection of heaven's empty promises. He chooses the mud over the mirage, the wound over the illusion of healing. This is faith stripped of reward—a leap into darkness with no net, no applause.

Modern parallels abound. Think of whistleblowers who choose truth over careers, activists who cling to hope in the face of futility, or a nurse holding the hand of a dying stranger in a pandemic. These are secular leaps of faith, moments where the absurd becomes sacred.

The Question: Can We Live Without Heaven?

The Mahabharata does not end with answers. Yudhishthira's test lingers like a half-remembered dream. Kierkegaard's leap, Camus' revolt, Nietzsche's amor fati—all converge here. To live ethically in an absurd world is to walk a tightrope between reason and madness, holding the hand of the forsaken.

The dog, now Dharma, whispers: "Heaven was never the point. The climb was."

The Descent – Faith as Rebellion

Heaven collapses like a stage set. Yudhishthira, crowned in ashes, walks away from the gods' theater. The dog—now Dharma—pads beside him, its fur shedding stars. Below, Earth spins, scarred and singing. The true test begins: to rule the absurd.

Modern Parables of Absurd Faith

1. The Nurse in the Pandemic:

She holds the hand of a stranger drowning in silence, knowing her PPE is tissue paper against fate. No angels applaud. No heaven waits. Her dharma is the grip of her glove, the weight of a breath.

2. The Whistleblower:

He leaks truths into the void, trading career for conscience. The world calls him traitor. The dog—loyalty—licks his wounds.

3. The Climate Activist:

She chains herself to a burning tree, howling into the ears of glaciers. No victory in sight. Her revolt is the act itself: I saw the void and planted a seed.

The Divine Joke Unmasked

Yudhishthira returns to a world where gods are algorithms, heaven a viral tweet. The dog becomes a stray on TikTok, limping through reels of curated joy. Dharma is not in temples but in the cracks—the unpaid janitor, the refugee's laugh, the quiet "no" to a corrupt deal.

Kierkegaard's leap is a daily chore now. Faith is choosing the dog again and again: the friend you call at 3 a.m., the protest you join knowing it won't trend, the love you nurture without guarantee.

The Final Sutra

The Mahabharata never ends. Yudhishthira's throne is your kitchen table. The dog waits. Will you betray it for a heaven of likes, promotions, and polished lies? Or will you sit on the floor, feed it scraps, and laugh at the sky's empty promises?

Heaven was the dog all along.

19. The Philosophy of Krishna

In the Mahabharata, Krishna emerges as a multidimensional figure—divine incarnate, diplomat, warrior, and philosopher. His teachings and actions, particularly in the Bhagavad Gita, offer a profound synthesis of ethics, metaphysics, and pragmatism. This essay explores Krishna's philosophy through the lens of global philosophical traditions, revealing how his ideas resonate with, challenge, and transcend frameworks from Kantian deontology to existentialism, while maintaining a uniquely holistic vision of duty, reality, and liberation.

Dharma and Deontology: Duty Beyond Desire

Krishna's central tenet in the Bhagavad Gita is dharma—one's righteous duty. When Arjuna hesitates to fight, Krishna admonishes him to act according to his svadharma (personal duty) as a warrior. This aligns with Immanuel Kant's deontology, where moral action derives from duty rather than consequences. For Kant, ethical acts adhere to universal maxims; similarly,

Krishna argues that Arjuna's duty (to uphold cosmic order) supersedes personal grief.

However, Krishna transcends Kant by contextualizing duty within guna (inherent nature) and karma (action). Unlike Kant's rigid universalism, Krishna's svadharma is fluid, tailored to one's role (e.g., a ruler's duty differs from a farmer's). This reflects Hegel's historical particularism, where ethics evolve through societal roles, yet Krishna anchors this in an eternal cosmic law (rita).

Nishkama Karma: The Stoic Art of Selfless Action

Krishna's doctrine of nishkama karma (action without attachment) mirrors Stoic equanimity and Epicurean ataraxia. He urges Arjuna to act without craving rewards, akin to Marcus Aurelius' call to "confine yourself to the present." Yet Krishna adds a theological layer: actions are offerings to the divine (Brahman), dissolving the ego's illusion.

This also parallels John Stuart Mill's utilitarianism, but with a critical twist. While Mill prioritizes outcomes, Krishna emphasizes intent: selfless action (sattvic) aligns with universal harmony, whereas outcome-driven motives (rajasic or tamasic) breed discord.

Here, Krishna synthesizes virtue ethics (Aristotle) with transcendental purpose.

The Self and the Absolute: Vedanta Meets Existentialism

Krishna's metaphysics revolve around the Atman (eternal self) and Brahman (universal consciousness). His teaching, "You are not the body, but the indestructible soul," echoes Plato's dualism, where the soul transcends the corporeal. Yet Krishna's non-dualistic Vedanta ("I am the Self in all beings") aligns more with Spinoza's pantheism, where divinity permeates existence.

Existentialist undertones emerge in Arjuna's crisis of meaning. While Sartre asserts "existence precedes essence," Krishna offers a divine essence: the self's unity with Brahman. Yet, like Kierkegaard's leap of faith, Krishna demands trust in the unseen cosmic order—a surrender (sharanagati) beyond rational proof.

The Vishvarupa: Cosmic Unity and Postmodern Relativity

In his theophany (Vishvarupa), Krishna reveals himself as the totality of creation and destruction. This vision aligns with Hegel's Absolute Spirit—the universe as a dynamic, interconnected whole—and Nietzsche's Dionysian chaos, where creation and destruction are inseparable.

Postmodern thinkers like Derrida might critique this as a "metanarrative," yet Krishna's form embodies quantum non-duality: opposites (life/death, good/evil) coexist as facets of the divine. His message—"I am time, the destroyer of worlds"—resonates with modern physics' entropy, framing morality within impermanence.

Pragmatism and Paradox: The Morality of War

Krishna's role in the Kuruksharata war sparks ethical debate. His tactical deceit (e.g., Bhishma's fall via Shikhandi, Karna's unarmed death) mirrors Machiavelli's realism: ends (cosmic justice) justify means. Yet Krishna, as divine arbiter, transcends human morality. His actions reflect moral particularism, where context—not rules—dictates ethics.

Critics like Gandhi question violence in service of dharma. However, Krishna distinguishes ahimsa (non-violence) from cowardice: when adharma dominates, righteous war (dharma yuddha) becomes duty. This prefigures Just War Theory, balancing proportionality and last resort.

Feminist and Feminist Critiques: Draupadi's Savior

Krishna's support for Draupadi during her disrobing highlights his commitment to justice, yet operates within a patriarchal framework. Feminist scholars like Judith Butler might critique his reliance on divine intervention over systemic change. However, his empowerment of marginalized voices (e.g., Vidura, Ekalavya) suggests a proto-intersectional ethic, valuing duty over caste.

Maya and Modernity: The Illusion of Certainty

Krishna's concept of maya (cosmic illusion) parallels Buddhist anicca (impermanence) and Schopenhauer's veil of perception. He teaches that attachment to the material world breeds suffering, urging detachment. This resonates with Heidegger's critique of inauthenticity, where societal roles obscure true selfhood.

Yet Krishna's maya is not nihilistic; it's a call to perceive the divine in the mundane, akin to Rumi's mystical poetry or Thoreau's transcendentalism.

Conclusion: The Philosopher-God

Krishna's philosophy defies categorization, weaving duty, metaphysics, and pragmatism into a tapestry of divine-human interplay. He is a Kantian deontologist in his emphasis on duty, a Stoic in his advocacy for equanimity, a Hegelian in his historical consciousness, and a mystic in his cosmic vision. Yet his uniqueness lies in harmonizing these strands into bhakti (devotion)—a path where love, action, and wisdom converge.

In an era of fragmented truths, Krishna's teachings remain a compass: act selflessly, perceive unity in diversity, and navigate moral complexity with courage and grace. As he declares in the Gita, "Where there is dharma, there is victory"—not of conquest, but of cosmic harmony.

Epilogue: The Eternal War Within

The Mahabharata is not an epic. It is a mirror. For 200,000 verses, it has held up a reflection to humanity's most primal questions: What is duty when the world burns? Can virtue survive violence? Does justice demand betrayal? Across these pages, we have wandered the Kurukshetra of the soul, where Pandavas and Kauravas are not kings and demons but the warring halves of our own fractured selves. This book, a humble attempt to decode an ancient codex through the prism of Western philosophy, has sought to illuminate a simple truth: the Mahabharata is not a story about them. It is a story about us.

The Unanswered Questions – And Why They Matter

You, the reader, have journeyed through chapters of paradoxes. You've seen Shantanu's grief dissected through Seneca's Stoicism, Draupadi's defiance refracted through Sartre's existentialism, and Karna's despair echo Nietzsche's nihilism. But perhaps you're left with more questions than answers:

- Can duty become tyranny? (Bhishma's vow vs. Kant's categorical imperative).

- Does victory justify deceit? (Krishna's pragmatism vs. Machiavelli's realism).

- Is identity a prison or a liberation? (Shikhandi's rebirth vs. Butler's performativity).

These are not flaws in the text. They are its purpose. The Mahabharata, like life, resists neat conclusions. It thrives in the liminal space between right and wrong, self and other, mortal and divine. This book has not sought to "solve" the epic but to unfold it—to show how its questions, when pressed against the forge of global philosophy, spark new fires of understanding.

The Mahabharata as a Philosophical Laboratory

The epic's genius lies in its refusal to reduce human experience to binaries. Consider:

1. Krishna – The Divine Pragmatist: He is Arjuna's charioteer, yet he steers the cosmos. His teachings in the Gita fuse Hegel's dialectics ("I am Time, the destroyer") with Kierkegaard's leap of faith ("Abandon all dharmas, surrender to me"). He is the ultimate synthesis: God as strategist, infinity as friend.

2. Draupadi – The Existentialist Queen: Her question, "Who owns me?" is a proto-feminist roar centuries before Beauvoir. Her disrobing is not victimhood but agency—a refusal to be reduced to property, even as the fabric of her sari stretches into eternity.

3. Karna – The Anti-Hero of Nihilism: Born a prince, raised a charioteer, he dies a paradox. His life asks: Can loyalty be a form of freedom? Camus' Sisyphus would nod; Nietzsche's Übermensch would salute.

These characters are not archetypes but lived philosophies. They bleed, doubt, and contradict themselves—and in doing so, they become more human than divine.

The Bridge Between Rivers: East, West, and the Ocean Beyond

This book began with a gamble: that the Mahabharata's dilemmas could converse with Plato's cave, Kant's imperatives, and Foucault's panopticon. Along the way, we found that:

- Stoicism's "acceptance" is mirrored in Vidura's silent suffering.

\- Marx's class struggle pulses in Ekalavya's severed thumb.

\- Heidegger's "being-toward-death" shudders in Arjuna's paralysis.

But the epic does more than mirror Western thought—it challenges it. Where Kant demands moral purity, Krishna endorses moral fluidity. Where Sartre declares, "Hell is other people," the Mahabharata whispers, "Hell is the self refusing to see itself in others."

This is not a clash of civilizations but a dialogue across time. The Mahabharata, like the Ganges, absorbs tributaries into its current. It reminds us that philosophy is not a fortress of ideas but a river—fluid, adaptable, life-giving.

The Modern Kurukshetra: Our Wars, Our Choices

Today's battles are fought not on fields of sand but in courtrooms, algorithms, and climate summits. Yet the Mahabharata's questions endure:

\- Climate Crisis: When Yudhishthira gambles his kingdom, he mirrors our leaders trading glaciers for

GDP. The epic asks: What will you sacrifice for short-term gain?

- AI Ethics: Shakuni's dice are algorithms now—opaque, manipulative, lethal. The epic warns: Beware those who reduce humanity to data.

- Identity Politics: Shikhandi's struggle to be seen resonates in transgender rights movements. The epic insists: The body is a vessel, not a verdict.

The Mahabharata does not offer solutions. It offers lenses—Hegelian, feminist, existential—to dissect our chaos. Its lesson is urgent: We are all Arjuna now, paralyzed between duty and despair, needing Krishna's clarity in a world of fake news and deepfakes.

The Unfinished Symphony

This book ends, but the Mahabharata does not. It spirals onward, a fractal of stories within stories. Yudhishthira's final test—choosing a stray dog over heaven—captures its essence: truth is not a destination but a direction. The dog, revealed as Dharma, is the ultimate paradox: divinity in the despised, wisdom in the wounded.

In our age of certitude, the epic's ambiguity is a gift. It teaches us to:

- Question absolutes (even this book's conclusions).

- Embrace contradictions (Karna's nobility in villainy).

- Seek unity in fragments (Krishna's Vishvarupa).

A Letter to the Reader

Dear Traveler,

You have crossed a vast terrain: from the icy grief of Shantanu to the molten rage of Bhima, from the despair of Karna to the quiet courage of Vidur. If this book has unsettled you—if its questions gnaw at your sleep, its paradoxes haunt your days—then it has succeeded.

The Mahabharata is not a relic. It is a living fire, passed from storyteller to listener for millennia. You are now its keeper. Carry its flames into boardrooms and bedrooms, protests and prayers. Let it burn away the dross of dogma, the rust of rigidity.

When faced with your own Kurukshetra—a moral dilemma, a heartbreak, a betrayal—remember:

- You are Arjuna, trembling but capable of greatness.

- You are Draupadi, defiant in the face of erasure.

- You are Krishna, weaving strategy from chaos.

And when all else fails, be the dog. The one who stays.

The Last Sutra

The Mahabharata ends with the Pandavas' ascent to heaven—a paradise that feels like punishment. Yudhishthira, the "righteous" king, finds his brothers in hell and his enemies in bliss. The gods laugh: "Did you think morality was arithmetic?"

This is the epic's final lesson: Life is not a equation to solve but a story to live. The answers you seek are not in these pages, or in any scripture, but in the choices you make when the dice fall, the crowd jeers, and the only voice left is your own.

So close this book. Step into your Kurukshetra. Fight your war.